DEAR PARENTS

LETTERS AND SPEECHES FROM A CHRISTIAN COACH TO FAMILIES

MATTHEW J. WUNDERLIN

WESTBOW
PRESS
A DIVISION OF THOMAS NELSON

WestBow Press books may be ordered through booksellers or by contacting:

WestBow Press
A Division of Thomas Nelson
1663 Liberty Drive
Bloomington, IN 47403
www.westbowpress.com
1-(866) 928-1240

ISBN: 978-1-4497-2066-7 (sc)
ISBN: 978-1-4497-2067-4 (hc)
ISBN: 978-1-4497-2065-0 (e)

Library of Congress Control Number: 2011932936

Printed in the United States of America

WestBow Press rev. date: 07/25/2011

To Parents

May you realize the precious responsibility given to you.

FOREWORD

"She knows it's a race, right?" we ask somewhat facetiously as our ten-year old daughter swims by, seemingly without a care in the world.

After the race, my eyes followed her as she walked over to Coach Matt to get the post-mortem on her backstroke event. I watched them confer, Matt all gestures and exclamations from afar, and I think to myself, "Wow, he's really laying into her." Then, I am surprised as her face breaks into a wide, beaming grin, and she skips back to us to report, "Coach Matt said that I 'shocked him,' and he doesn't shock very easily. I took 5 seconds off of my personal best time!" An onlooker might have guessed that she'd won a blue ribbon, rather than finished in last place.

My daughter swims better than 90% of the planet, according to Coach. But realistically, I know that she'll never be an Olympic swimmer. Fellow parents, if we're honest with ourselves, very few of our children will ever achieve that level of swimming.

Coach Matt would answer that assertion with the following: "It's not about being an Olympian. It's about *being Olympian*...learning to be a hero. And, it's not comfortable to be a hero. If it were, being one wouldn't be so great."

Coach Matt stresses the importance of "making good people, not just good swimmers," through dedication to the five Orcas values of sportsmanship, spirit, motivation, dedication and excellence. It was this whole-person approach to swimming that led my family to join the Waunakee Orcas in 2008.

Upon enrollment, my family began to receive informational email from Coach Matt. The parent letters contained within these pages began as a way to pass on information about practices, schedules and meets, but soon they morphed into Coach Matt morsels of swim techniques, anecdotes and philosophies. His letters, one part daily devotional and one part parenting handbook, have a Paul Harvey, "The Rest of the Story" appeal.

As a parent, I enjoyed receiving these little life lessons, and found myself, not only contemplating them days later, but also sending them onto other friends and family.

Often I received commentary back from the recipients that included words like "positive," "inspirational," and "motivational." Some parents lamented that they wished that their kids' coaches were like Coach Matt. Others wanted to know if they could get on the Orcas mailing list, even if they didn't have a swimmer in the family. And still others mentioned, "I wish Coach Matt was my (fill-in-the-blank) dad, brother, friend, Coach."

I am grateful to call Coach Matt my friend. But I am even more blessed that my daughter received his guidance and tutelage as a swimming coach for several years. I hope that his inspirational messages enhance your lives as they have ours.

Deb Nies

CONTENTS

Introduction

Dear Reader,

The following is a compilation of letters and speeches that I wrote for the Waunakee Orcas of Wisconsin (WOW) swim team I coached between 2006 and 2011. The letters have been cut down (because you probably don't care whether or not the children needed fins on Thursday), and edited for clarification and to expand on a few points. However, what you will read is largely what was sent to families over the years.

You may be curious as to how these letters came about – that is, why would a swimming coach send these to parents on his team? Well, many coaches send weekly or monthly newsletters to their families in order to keep communication open and to summarize what is going on in the program. I decided this was very important to our new team. Then, since we decided we wanted to be a values-based organization, I began to add little stories and snippets to the weekly newsletter which reflected my philosophy on sports – my philosophy being a Christian perspective.

Almost immediately I began to receive positive feedback for this portion of the newsletter. People were forwarding my letters to friends, sharing them with their children, and using them to benefit their lives. For many, it was something they looked forward to. I couldn't believe it, and I praised God for the opportunity to share.

After several years, I started to receive encouragement from people to compile these letters into a book. My initial thought was to "cut-and-paste" my musings into a PDF document and give it to the families on Orcas. Then I received further encouragement to make it into something that can reach a larger audience, as the truths here apply to a much larger audience than what I was reaching.

To be honest, I was very intimidated by this task, however things continued to fall into place until I truly felt it was God's will for me to actually make this into a book. Though my sport is swimming, this will truly benefit any coach or parent participating in any sport.

One thing to note is that I typically read a book or two per week and many people have forwarded me "inspirational" emails over the years. I cannot claim credit for every idea in these letters, but there is no way at this point I can figure out where the ideas included in my letters came from. That said, the writing is my own and not plagiarism. To those unknown authors who have helped me mature and who have provided me with stepping stones for inspiration in these letters, "Thank you."

My prayer, dear reader, is that you will enjoy what is written here and that you will use it for your edification. I pray that if there is anything in these pages which is not honoring to God and the truth of scripture that you will ignore it.

My final request is that if you are touched by the following letters that you will refer this book to others. As a new author, and as someone who is, quite frankly, not good at marketing, I am counting on you to encourage others to get this book to grow in their faith and in their lives.

Sincerely,

Coach Matt
March 2011

THERE IS A STORY OF…

1

One of my favorite stories is that of Roger Bannister. I'm sure for most of you this name is familiar, even if you can't place it. He was a runner. Back in the 1950s, many of the world's top doctors and physiologists believed that human beings had reached their maximum potential in the mile race. Most believed it was IMPOSSIBLE to go faster than four minutes in the mile – that the human heart would actually explode in the attempt. It simply couldn't be done because the body would shut down in an effort to protect itself. The goal of most world class runners was to get as close to that four-minute mark as possible.

Then on May 6, 1954 Roger Bannister did the impossible – he ran a mile in 3:59.4. Not even two months later, two other individuals ran even faster, advancing the world record to 3:58.0. So what happened to the physical barrier that prevented humans from running the four minute mile? Was there a sudden leap in training technique or had we changed genetically?

No. It was the change in THINKING that made the difference. Bannister had shown that breaking a four-minute mile was possible. Often the barriers we perceive are only barriers in our own minds. Previous runners had been held back by their beliefs and mindsets. When the barrier was broken, other runners saw that is was possible.

To date, from the best records that I can find, 955 runners have run sub-four-minute miles. What experts KNEW couldn't be done has now been done over 4,700 times!

Our beliefs and mindsets limit or expand our world. Beliefs have power over us because we treat them as though they're true. Beliefs influence what you attempt or choose not to attempt in life. They determine what you pay attention to, how you react to difficult situations, and ultimately, your attitude. Success and failure begin and end in what the mind believes is possible. The first step we can take in influencing the world around us is to change how we think about it. Just like the runners of time past, many of the barriers that hold us back today exist only in our minds.

Once you believe AND work hard AND sacrifice while pursuing your belief, it doesn't matter if you win, lose, or drop dead at the finish line because in the end, you will not regret it because now you know exactly who you are.

By the way, the current world record in the mile is 3:43.13.

2

There once was a great piano player who filled concert halls wherever he went. One night before his performance, in which he was to play a number of complicated pieces, a young man approached him.

"Sir, I wish I could perform in a place like this. I want to play in front of thousands just like you do."

The accomplished musician paused, then looked at the young man and said, "Today, I will grant you your wish. I will tell everyone that I'm not feeling well and that you are going to play in my stead."

The young man was shocked, "But sir, I can't do that! There is no way I can do what you do."

"That is because though you now have the opportunity, you don't have the freedom."

I like this story because it applies to the sport of swimming and to many other areas of life. Every single swimmer on our team has the opportunity to swim at the state meet this year. In fact, every swimmer has the opportunity to make the Olympic Trials. There are no rules preventing them; there are no people trying to stop them; there are no barriers in their way that others don't also have to deal with. The opportunity is available to everyone.

However, most don't have the freedom to swim at either meet.

All too often in life we limit ourselves by not putting in the effort to get what we want. We have taken away our own freedom by wasting time on things like watching television, playing video games, spreading ourselves too thin with other activities, simply being lazy, or doing a myriad of other things where our time could be used more wisely. There are three reasons why this often happens.

The first reason is that many people don't consciously know what they want, so they don't know what to prepare for. These are the most enslaved. They wander without purpose and life passes them by. Everyone needs to develop goals if they want the freedom to be great.

The second problem is that once people know what they want, many aren't willing to sacrifice in order to get it. Either they think the world owes them or they try to do the minimum to get by. Later they whine about how they didn't get what they wanted even though, on the surface, they "did what they were supposed to." Those who are great, regardless of endeavor, always look for ways to do more. Michael Phelps practices on Christmas.

The third reason is that many people start out the right way and then let circumstances control them. There isn't an Olympian anywhere who didn't have to deal with injury, getting sick, tragedy, too much homework, family problems, being too tall or to short, and every other excuse we use to justify our failures. The difference is that they chose to not let these "reasons" get in their way.

3

In the spring of 1519 Hernando Cortez led a fleet of 11 ships from Spain to the new world. Life was hard for the European explorers. They were in a strange land, far away from home and loved ones. There were fears of disease, food shortages, and a host of other problems that we don't need to go into. As can be imagined, there was a lot of grumbling and negativity and hopelessness. In short, many of them wanted to go home before the expedition had hardly even begun.

A group of the explorers planned a mutiny, but before they could pull it off, Cortez did something remarkable – he ordered the ships to be burned. As the ships burned so did thoughts of mutiny. Now, they had only two options – succeed in their mission or die.

When Cortez gave the order to burn the ships, his men no doubt "got it" that he was serious about this mission. Negative thoughts disappeared with the ships. They had to. Last Saturday, I asked your children to 'burn the ships' and remove any negative thoughts that they may be holding on to about swimming and commit themselves to doing the very best they could. The results of the meet showed that they did. A group of children showed what could happen when you remove negativity and commit to something.

As I've said before, your children never cease to amaze me.

It takes commitment equal to Cortez burning the ships if you really want results. If you want to be a world class swimmer, you must commit to swimming. If you want to be the best you can be in anything, you must commit to that. Even if you want to do something simple like "stop biting your nails," you have to remove the option to fail. And it all starts in the mind.

But in today's world, what is a typical commitment made by most people? All too often it's a lukewarm response that says, "Sure, I can give it a shot." We only pretend to commit because of our fears of failure (or success). Then we look busy by "trying to run to second base while keeping our foot on first."

We all go through times in our lives when we know we must commit to some new goal or challenge. To do this we need to make changes. And if we are honest, we will admit it scares the daylights out of us. We all want the potential reward and excitement that change offers, and there's often real excitement in our voice when we talk about the challenge. But we don't want to put forth the effort and the sacrifice and the drudgery of working hard day after day once the glory of talking about our goals has died.

It's easy and fun to make resolutions; it's hard to get out of bed in the morning to make them a reality. And that's why some people go their whole lives without ever reaching a goal. Commitment requires real action; the kind of action Cortez took when he gave the order, "Burn the ships."

Fully committing to success means there are no excuses. Simply saying "I want to do this or that" isn't good enough. We may have thoughts or lifestyle patterns that have once benefited us in the past, but now only serve as a hindrance. They must be burned.

Burn the ship of options and excuses and make a real commitment! No more "woulda," "coulda" or "shoulda" and no mindset of "I will go down fighting." I will not go down fighting, because I will not fail! If you want to win, don't allow losing to be an option. Victory comes with the commitment that is willing to "burn the ships."

This applies to our faith as well. We cannot commit to a new life in Christ if we're trying to hold onto our old self with its bad habits. We must not give ourselves the option to fail! We are "doulos," slaves to Christ when we believe in him. There are no choices for slaves. There is no other alternative to serving and doing God's will. Commit and burn the ships!

4

There is a story about a young man who was going to be mentored by a wise old sage. He approached the wise individual and not knowing what to say, asked him, "Sir, what are we going to do today?" The sage replied, "The same thing we will do every day – the best we can."

One of our philosophies in Orcas is "Excellence". We believe that excellence is achieved by aspiring to master our other mission statements: "spirit," "sportsmanship," "dedication," and "motivation." Our goal with Orcas is that our mission statement will carry beyond the pool and positively affect your child in all areas of their life. We are always glad when a child becomes a fast swimmer, but we are most proud when we see a child transform into a responsible young lady or gentleman.

But, in sports this will not happen on its own. It must be deliberately taught. There are too many elite athletes who are bad role models. There are too many coaches willing to sell their integrity for a few extra points. There are too many people (including parents) who look at winning as being the most important thing. There are too many people whose self-esteem is based entirely on how they perform in a recreational pastime.

This is a problem. And I know of no other way to fix it than to get back to the basics and constantly remind people of the values taught in the Bible. To do the best we can every day, we must go back to the instruction manual.

5

In the early days of the Berlin Wall, when emotions were still very much on edge and hostility was running high, truckloads of garbage were dumped over the wall from the eastern sector onto the western side. Everyone in West Berlin was outraged at such a terrible deed. How to best get revenge was the topic of conversation on every street corner, in every home.

Mayor Willie Brandt issued word that every flower, every petal, every bit of green that could be gathered was to be brought to an appointed spot at the wall. All of that beauty and fragrance was thrown over the wall to the eastern sector, and above the wall a great banner was hoisted. As the banner was unfurled, these words were revealed: "Each gives what he has." The East German government had thrown garbage; the West German people threw back flowers.

The Orca Way value of "excellence" can be summed up in those five words: Each gives what he has. If spirit, sportsmanship, dedication, and motivation are strived for, the result will be excellence – both in our sport and in life. If you are filled with negative things, regardless of possible short term successes, in the long run what is inside of you will be seen.

May we all strive to be excellent by filling ourselves with what matters, and not those things that distract or otherwise inhibit us.

6

Congratulations on two successful swim meets this past week! Between the two, we had more personal bests than I could count. You should be very proud of your children. Additionally, at the meet, another coach told me that they loved our team because of our swimmers' politeness. As a coach, that means more to me than any amount of blue ribbons and trophies. Let's keep up the good work!

Some of you may have heard this story before, but as we wind down to the last month of the season, it bears repeating.

In the early 1900s, a man by the name of Charles Daniels attended a swim meet in New York and traveled 100 meters in 1:03.6. This time is not super impressive, but consider the conditions under which he swam. First, it was done in a frog pond with no turns, no lane lines or gutters, and he couldn't see 10 feet in front of his face. Second, he trained only 3 times per week and no more than 800 meters per session. Finally, he wore a full length body suit, from ankles to shoulders, made of *wool*.

NOW, this story seems quite remarkable. The only thing Mr. Daniels did have was excellent form and technique.

It is easy, as we start to focus on goals, to forget the little things that got us to where we are in the first place. On the swim team, it is our technique; in other parts of life it may be sincerity, integrity, another person's sacrifice, or going the extra mile for someone else.

There is no such thing as "not a big deal." Every flip turn matters because you are creating a habit. Every bit of gossip matters because you hurt someone and build up a callous to sin. As we grow older we often think that the "basics" are just for kids. Yet, I challenge you to reexamine yourself as to how you act compared to what you value. You may be surprised.

We are never too old to outgrow the need for self-examination and discipline in the small things. Swimmers work on refining their technique their entire career because otherwise it starts to slip. We *must* constantly work on our values for the same reason, and even more so now that we are parents for the sake of matching our actions with what we want to teach our children.

If you do the little things well, the big things tend to take care of themselves.

7

I'm sure many of you know that Leonardo da Vinci was quite a prolific artist. Nearly every painting he did could be classified as a masterpiece. What you may not know is that as you page through the 13,000 pages of his sketch books that you will find hundreds of sketches of just hands and numerous sketches of just eyes and faces etc.

There are a lot of "one hit wonders" out there, but in order to make a habit of creating masterpieces, one must first master the details.

John Leonard, head of the American Swim Coach Association, estimates the minimum time for a swimmer to reach their maximum potential is 9400 hours of DELIBERATE practice. "Deliberate practice" means that they are doing the workout as the workout was designed (proper intensity, correct stroke, kicking, always doing flip turns, etc.), and they also consciously chose something they personally want to improve every moment of practice, so that they get a fraction better every day (tighter streamline, earlier catch, faster flip, getting more repetitions in dry land, proper head position while breathing, etc.).

It is this sort of mentality that should guide our practices. And it is this sort of mentality that I hope will help your children in all aspects of life. This way, when opportunity arrives, we are free to take advantage of it by having prepared.

8

A carpenter had worked long and hard for many years and was ready to retire. He told his employer. His boss knew this sad day would come, and asked the carpenter if he could just build one more house as a personal favor.

The carpenter agreed, but it was obvious that his heart was not in his work. He resorted to cutting corners and using inferior materials. He did the bare minimum to meet the code requirements, and only met the minimum standards of quality.

When the carpenter finished his work, the employer came and handed him the keys to the front door. "This is your house," the employer said, "your reward for all that you have done."

Whether in swimming or in life, we live in the house that we have built. Every day we hammer a nail, place a board, or erect a wall. Our attitude and the choices we make determine whether we live in a mansion or a shack. Being physically present, but not showing up, is the quickest way to find frustration and disappointment, regardless of your endeavor.

A coach, like the employer, can provide blueprints and oversee the project, but only the swimmer, like the carpenter, can actually build the house. Every person needs a higher authority and ideals to which he or she is accountable. Every swimmer needs a set of principles to which they adhere in order to maximize potential.

Our team has the Orca Values which are based on parts of the book of Romans in the Bible. But intellectual agreement isn't enough – it must be followed by action. This is why the book of James says that "Faith without works is dead."

It is not enough to say you are going to build a quality house, you have to actually do it by acting consistent with your faith!

9

One thing we talked about last week was the importance of integrity. I shared with your children the story of Jerry Mita who returned over $2,450,000 to the state of Utah, when they mistakenly input most of his social security number into the amount owed instead of the $15 he was supposed to get. (By the way, nobody from any of the groups correctly guessed what Jerry did with the money—although one child said "he invested the money, doubled it, and then returned the $2 million.")

In swimming, it is vital that we do the right thing all of the time even when coach isn't looking, because it helps us form good habits. Also, our teammates are counting on us to have done everything possible to prepare for races and relays. What you do in practice is what you will do in a meet.

This is true of life, as well. Who you are when you don't think anyone is watching is who you REALLY are. God is always watching and knows your heart. He often uses life's circumstances to reveal our character to ourselves. He does this using both prosperity and adversity.

Oddly enough, it seems that we fail the test of prosperity more than the test of adversity. We grow through our struggles but stagnate in our blessings. We focus on doing the right thing more when situations are difficult than when they are abundant. I think it is because we confuse God's test for a reward when prosperity comes, and we try to get rewarded by "being good" when adversity comes.

We forget that, ultimately, the reward for doing the right thing is having done it. Every other good thing we get is just grace.

10

There is the story of an elevator operator who worked in a large sky rise, and every day he filled the car with whistling.

One day an executive, who was having a particularly bad day, asked him what on earth he could possibly be whistling about.

He replied, "Well sir, I ain't never lived today before."

Each day has new opportunities to be seized and new lessons to be learned. With hard work and effort comes learning and improvement. I think the children realized that this weekend. This type of realization leads to wonderful things.

Parents play a very crucial role in their child's athletic development. Because of that, we decided it would be beneficial for me to give a little talk to the team on some sports psychology issues. I plan to speak a bit about how the mind works, mindsets people get into, motivation, and how to develop talent. As a teaser: Most of what we call "talent" comes from hard work, not innate capability. In a very real way, it is something that can be created and developed. Your role as a parent is even more critical in this regard than my role as a coach.

Each day your child lives is a day they have never lived before either. They need your guidance to grow as athletes and human beings. Raising your children in the ways "they should go" is your number one biblical responsibility.

11

Former Secretary of Defense Donald Rumsfeld had an interesting quirk. He had all of his desks made to be at a height where, in order to do his work, he had to stand behind them. When asked why he did this, he responded, "If I get too comfortable sitting around I won't get anything done. When I stand, I am just going to take care of business and move on to the next thing."

This is true of all of us too. When we are comfortable, we have no motivation to move on or do anything else. Think about the last time you were on vacation and didn't want to get out of that beach chair!

Today I want to talk a little bit about why reducing comfort and delaying gratification produces motivation.

We all know that our children "have it good." They have it so good because we desire the best for them. But some of our appropriate intentions may backfire when it comes to producing motivation. If your child has everything he wants, he will not go out in search of things. If what he wants is just given to him, he will never learn how to pursue those wishes. A child who has whatever he desires without earning it, will never learn how to prioritize.

Reducing comfort creates motivation that results in gaining experience and perspective, which will one day fuel a purpose. As such, it is good to eliminate some comforts. As the parent it is your decision as to what your child should do without for his own good and for the good of your family.

Now, we do not want to entirely eliminate all comforts, so what should we do? First, it is beneficial to wait. If your child will "just die if they don't get new boots by next week," it is our job as parents to show her that she is incorrect. Second, there things they may want which they can and should earn. Cell phones are great, but why should parents pay for it? If you want to produce motivation, see what happens if your child has to pay for half (or all) of her monthly bill. Waiting for things and learning how to earn them will teach patience and gratefulness. Learning how to get what they desire helps children prioritize desires and learn how to distinguish between wants and needs.

There can be no motivation if all needs and desires are met. In our society, we can still give our children a lifestyle most kings throughout history could only dream of, without sacrificing their motivation.

12

I want to share with you a little story about integrity that happened on our team this past week. I am going to keep the swimmer anonymous, but be assured the swimmer's parents were informed.

As many of you know, we do star charts for the yellow, red, and white groups. Essentially we test the children on a variety of skills; if they complete a skill successfully they get a star to put with the skill completed, and once all the skills on their sheet have a star by them, they are ready to advance to the next practice group level.

Stars are pretty difficult to get, and most swimmers recognize that it is a "big deal" to get one.

After practice, this young swimmer approached me looking very concerned. "Coach," this athlete said, "I got a star but I didn't do the skill right." Now, we watch the athletes pretty closely so I asked this individual what they did wrong. After the explanation was complete, it was true this swimmer did something wrong that nobody saw – they were supposed to touch the wall with two hands simultaneously, but this person "kind of touched with one hand a little bit before the other one."

This reminded me of two quotes: "Integrity is doing the right thing, even if nobody is watching." "We notice the loss of integrity when people act immorally in a substantial way, but the reality is that it is lost one seemingly insignificant compromise at a time."

How true that is, and how much we can learn from a little child who decided that a star is not worth the loss of character.

13

In Dostoevsky's book, "The Idiot," the central character, Prince Myshkin, is thrust into a culture obsessed with wealth, power, and lust. But the prince himself has no pride, no greed, no malice, no envy, no vanity, and no fear. His behavior is so abnormal that people do not know what to think of him. On the one hand, they trust him because of his innocence and simplicity, yet his lack of ulterior motives causes them to conclude that he must be an idiot.

Dostoevsky skillfully weaves the themes of money, power, and lust throughout the story, contrasting the spirit of the prince with those around him. Of course, the real question throughout the story is, who really is the idiot? Most would conclude that the true fool is the person whose life is dominated by greed, power, and lust.

My temptation as a coach is to try to be more like the teams around us. Your children's temptation will be to be more like the athletes around them, and like the ones seen on television. After all, if everyone wants to be consumed with glory, competitiveness, and self-aggrandizement it can't be all bad. Right?

Wrong.

One of the values on our team is "spirit." Of all the values we have, I think this one separates us most from the rest of the teams out there. It is the spirit that every swimmer matters, not just those on the A relays or those going to state. It is the spirit that you can have a life outside of the pool and still be just as much of a valuable teammate. It is the spirit that how you do something is more important than what you do, within reason. It is the spirit that swimming is better utilized as a tool for helping children become better people, than an end with a focus on merely making a better athlete.

Be sure to remind your children of what is most important in life. It is easy to get caught up in the momentum that Orcas is growing, we are able to compete against the best schools in the state, and that we compete well against other individuals not just ourselves. But as the Bible says, "What good is it for a person to gain the whole world, and yet lose or forfeit his very self?"

We must be ever vigilant of what makes us Orcas . . . and not everybody else.

14

I heard a great (true) story this week that has some good lessons I want to share with you.

A few years ago Japanese grocery stores were experiencing a problem. Stores in Japan are much smaller than our stores and so they have no space to waste. The Japanese people love watermelons (as does everyone I would imagine!), but watermelons, being big and round, waste a lot of space. Because of this, most stores don't carry them in that crowded country.

Most people would tell you that watermelons grow round and there is nothing that can be done about it. But some Japanese farmers took a different approach. If grocery stores don't like round watermelons, why don't we give them square watermelons?

Now, I'm sure there were many scoffers, but it wasn't long before they invented square watermelons. The solution to the problem of "watermelons are round" wasn't nearly as difficult to solve for those who didn't assume at the start the problem was impossible. They simply starting questioning usual methods and found a creative solution that made grocery stores happy. It had the added benefit that it was easier and more cost effective to ship. I'm also sure people were pleased that it took up less refrigerator space as well.

How did they do it? As it turns out, all you need to do to grow a square watermelon is to put them in boxes while they are growing, and the watermelon will take on the shape of the box.

But there are three levels even deeper than that to explain "how did they do it" which can help in all areas of life. The first level is we can't just assume something. Most things we do, we do so habitually that we can't imagine there is another way. Breaking the habit of "assumption" can help us improve, as we constantly look for ways to solve a problem. This is hard because many of the assumptions we make, we don't even realize we are making.

The second level is to question habits. This will help us with number one. Forming habits when they are well thought out is usually a very positive thing, but most of us have adopted a majority of our habits from various people, places, and times without even thinking about them. I bet that we have no idea where a majority of our habits even came from! By questioning our habits, we can make life more enjoyable, instead of always defaulting to the way things are now.

The third level is to be creative until a solution presents itself. Now, many of us "assume" and fall back on the "habit" of saying "I'm not a creative person." You don't have to be an artist to look at things from another perspective, and the more you look at things from a different perspective, the more creative you will become in finding solutions to problems.

Homework for the week: Find something you can't do, but wish you could (swimming or otherwise). Now assume that you can do it or that you have to do it, and ask yourself "how can I do this" or "is there a better way for me to go about doing this?" Be creative in coming up with solutions and throw nothing out.

Realize that impossibilities often aren't.

15

Last weekend, completely by accident, I had a great moment in parenting. We were visiting my parents who live on a farm in Southwest Wisconsin. My father has bad shoulders, so when my brothers and I visit, we usually help dad out doing the things he can no longer easily do. Last week, I brought the kids with me.

On the car ride home, after almost three days on the farm, I asked the children what they enjoyed the most. Titus, my three year old, quickly stated, "When I helped you unload wood." Bryce, who is five, said, "When I helped you feed the calves." And Sierra, who is eight, said, "When we cut the tree up." The commonality was that it was all work and it was all work they did with me. Now, they played, watched movies, ate candy, and enjoyed lots of other entertainment while they were visiting their grandparents. But their favorite part was work. I began to wonder if my children were okay.

Then I realized something: Little people want to grow up and be like big people. And the big people they most want to be like are their parents. We all work. Work is where we learn perseverance and discipline. Work can be fun, and we develop a sense of accomplishment through doing it. It seems that all work and no play may make John a dull boy, but all play and no work can also be harmful.

Work is also an investment. The jobs I did with my kids only took about fourteen times as long, because I had them with me and actually let them help. But think also of the rewards – They learned how to help and be productive. They also learned they can be helpful and needed. They bonded with me over a common task. They learned some common sense, and they grew in confidence. Those things won't happen over entertainment or by being coddled. There is no short cut to maturity, and you can't gain experience from a book or a television set.

Many people have issues with work even when it is play. In swim practice we work, but really, it is a form of play. In basketball, hockey, choir, theater, drawing class, etc. there is a lot of work, but in actuality, it is recreation and fun. What is valuable is that these activities still teach life skills like discipline, perseverance, etc. But it is scary to think that many people won't even work for fun. So what will happen as they grow older?

In the Bible, Adam and Eve tended the garden *before* the fall. From that, we should take the lesson that work is a blessing, not a curse. It is even more of a blessing when your children are at your side and after an exhausting weekend say, "Look what WE did together."

16

One of our team's mantras is "Excellence is a habit." While excellence gets recognized in meets and competitions, it is created over the weeks, months, and years of practice. You have heard it said that "practice makes perfect" but in reality only "perfect practice makes perfect." If you practice something poorly, you cannot expect perfection in the moments when it really matters.

This is true of life as well. This week I used an example for the kids about why you need to be excellent all of the time; why 90% of the time isn't good enough. Imagine that you have to have heart surgery. It is a grim thought, but, for the sake of discussion, pretend that you have visited your surgeon and are pretty happy with him.

Then the day of the operation comes. A nurse is getting you ready for your operation. As she begins to wheel you into the operating room she says, "Oh, you are going to love this doctor. He does 90% of everything really well. Sometimes he isn't so good at certain things because he's tired or doesn't feel like it. But he's really good most of the time."

Few would find reassurance with this statement. Few would feel this doctor was a true professional. Nobody would say that he is excellent.

Yet this is the mentality we use all too often - that what we're doing is "good enough." Then we are surprised when we don't improve, get rewarded, or even accomplish what we set out to do. Swimming is a great sport to achieve a mindset that can bring about excellence in life, and that is why we want to focus on excellence in all of the "little things" this season.

17

One day when my daughter was two-years old, I walked into our bedroom and saw her standing on top of our dresser.

Immediately, being the good father that I am (oh, yes, I was supposed to be watching her), I asked Sierra, "What in the world are you doing?"

"I want to see if I can jump from here onto the bed," came her sweet reply.

"Sweetie, that's crazy. You could get badly hurt," I responded.

It was nearly four feet to the ground, and the bed was a good three or four feet from the dresser. I wasn't even sure how she got up there.

After surveying the scene I continued, "You need to put some pillows or cushions down on the floor first, so that if you miss you'll have a softer landing."

Alright, so maybe that won't win me father-of-the-year, but this week I want to talk a bit about the importance of letting our children take risks. Now, I'm not talking about letting them do anything and everything, or about taking off the helmets or knee pads (or jump off dressers), rather I would like to demonstrate that controlled risk-taking is an important part of producing motivation.

Our children have very few risks in their environment compared to what we had growing up. We live in an age with plenty of food, safety equipment, health care, and cell phones. There are numerous education programs that talk about safety. There is no doubt that safety is important, but children need to take chances in order to develop common sense, risk management skills, and to mature in general.

With risk comes the chance to fail. This is its benefit to motivation. A person cannot strive for success if they are forever in fear of failure. They cannot learn how to grow, and learn from mistakes, if they are never allowed the chance to fail. Finding a purpose for your life or pursuing any worthwhile goal involves a great deal of risk. Risk teaches children to get out of their comfort zone for what is truly important.

During swim practice, there is a big risk when you work as hard as you can: What if I can't make it through the set? What if I "die?" What if I get hurt? What if others still beat me? What if I get too tired? What if I just can't do it?

If your child never takes controlled risks, they will be crippled by something as simple as the decision to work hard in a swimming practice. How much more will they be crippled someday when it really matters?

Without risk and the possibility of failure, no one can move toward something meaningful.

18

D r. Hardial Singh Sainbhy of India has an interesting distinction. He holds the world record for the most non-honorary degrees. Currently, he has 35 degrees, of which 15 are Master's degrees and five others are also at the postgraduate level.

This seemed impressive to me, and as I researched his life, I found that the accounts of his educational accomplishments were filled with accolades. In reading about this man, I discovered one lone dissenter who concluded that this man was completely wasting his life.

Why? The commenter didn't say, but I think we all recognize that knowledge without action is wasted. Knowledge without wisdom is tragedy.

Does Dr. Sainbhy act on his knowledge? I don't know. It seems there is little time to act long enough to make a significant impact when he is so immersed in gaining more initials after his name. Is Dr. Sainbhy wise? I don't know the answer to that question either. However, if he feels the purpose of life is to acquire more slips of paper with his name on it, then I would question how much wisdom he has.

I know swimmers who have all of the right knowledge. They can talk about how to do everything correctly. They can answer all of the coaches' questions. When we recommend a corrective action to them they respond "I know."

I often respond, "Don't tell me you know, show me!"

Our swimmers will not improve in the sport if their knowledge isn't acted upon. They must convert that knowledge into action if they are to respect themselves, their team, and their sport. Certainly, nobody will consider them wise for failing to use that knowledge. Any failure is their fault and their responsibility. It is sad how a little laziness can lead to wasted practices and wasted opportunities.

That said, let me ask you parents a couple of difficult questions: How many of you know you should spend more time with your children? How many of you know you owe somebody an apology? How many of you know you should end some type of habit or behavior? How many of you know you are neglecting your religious duties? How many of you know what you need to do to reach your goal? How many of you know how you should treat your spouse? How many of you know that you spend too much time or money on trivial things? How many of you know you are neglecting some truth?

And when someone reaches the end of their season, career, or life, there will be no one who pities or respects the person who didn't act on what they know.

19

The Washington Post recently organized an experiment in a Washington D.C. subway station. They had one of the best musicians in the world, Joshua Bell, play some of the most intricate violin pieces ever written for approximately 45 minutes. He played these pieces on his violin worth $3.5 million dollars. Two days before playing in that subway station, Mr. Bell had sold out a theater in Boston where seats averaged $100.

It was calculated that thousands of people passed through this particular station during the time of the experiment, most on their way to work. What kind of crowd do you think was drawn by this once-in-a-lifetime opportunity?

Of the thousands that passed by, only six stopped to listen – most were children who were then, without exception, urged to move on by their parents. Twenty people gave him tips, totaling $32, as they walked by at their normal pace.

Do we perceive beauty in our everyday environment? Can we recognize talent in unexpected places? How much greatness do we miss in life, simply because we don't pay attention?

As we continue together in this journey of life, I want to encourage everyone to slow down a bit and enjoy what is happening around you. Live in the moment so that you don't miss out on the wonderful gifts God has placed around you.

20

Most of us are vaguely familiar with Napoleon's "Battle of Waterloo." When Napoleon returned to power, a large force assembled against the emperor. The leaders of that force were expecting him to resume his empire building. Napoleon feared his country being invaded and decided that the best defense was to take the offense. Thus, the three-day Battle of Waterloo began on June 16, 1815. Napoleon was defeated for the final time, and this loss put an end to his rule as Emperor.

Today, someone's Waterloo is a euphemism for his decisive or crushing defeat.

Much of the truth of this defeat has been forgotten. It was not the overwhelming victory that results seem to indicate. In fact, the Duke of Wellington, who won the battle, called it "the nearest run thing you ever saw in your life." It was practically a tie.

Many military historians point out that a three hour delay by the French army is what cost Napoleon the victory. On June 18, 1815 Napoleon delayed attacking Wellington's army until noon while he waited for the ground to dry. Those few extra hours of waiting gave the Prussian army enough time to arrive and break through his right flank. Ultimately, this caused the French army to waive the white flag.

Three hours were the difference between certain victory and absolute defeat.

I like this bit of history because three hours is essentially one day of swim practice.

It is easy to think that skipping a workout won't matter that much. It is easy to think that you'll get to learn something another time. It is easy to think that a few hours squandered won't make a difference in your life.

Yet three hours was important enough that it cost Napoleon the country of France. If it can cost someone something so huge, it can cost us dearly in less significant matters, as well.

In the case of the Battle of Waterloo it is easy to connect the dots in hindsight. It seems foolish for Napoleon to make that decision to waste that time...now. But in preparing for the future, we don't know how the dots are going to connect. Are you willing to risk that which you will never get back - time and opportunity?

We don't know what may or may not happen with the moments we thought didn't matter. Seize your opportunities NOW so that you can avoid your own personal Waterloo.

21

I heard a great story this week that I thought I'd share with you.

When Ty Cobb turned 70 years old he was interviewed by Larry King.

Larry King asked the Hall of Famer, "What do you think you'd hit if you were playing these days?"

Cobb, who still holds the lifetime batting average of .367, said, "About .290, maybe .300."

"That's because of the travel, the night games, the artificial turf, and all the new pitches like the slider, right?" King asked.

"No," responded Cobb, "it's because I'm seventy."

At times, we could all use that type of confidence! But that kind of confidence doesn't just come by virtue of belief. It comes as a result of lots of hard work and knowing that you did all you could to master yourself.

We live in a world where many people believe that self-esteem comes BEFORE great performances. There is a confusion of cause and effect. The reality is that self-esteem is created when we actually accomplish something. It is destroyed by artificial praise.

This has led to many problems in our world, including our churches. Many people don't like to talk about sin and hell because they are difficult subjects. To that I respond, "How can you understand the good news if you don't realize there is also bad news?"

If your child is not being responsible we can't assume it is because low self-esteem and then artificially try to tell them they are "fine just the way they are." They are not fine the way they are. They are sinful, just like everybody else! They need to be told the truth so that they will change.

They need to understand reality so that can gain confidence and self-esteem by actually earning it!

22

A study was done on a group of inner city youth. The school followed the children through their high school years (even if they didn't graduate high school) and into adulthood. The researchers found what they expected: drug addicts, single family homes, and unemployed individuals living off of government subsidies.

But they noticed there was a pocket of individuals who were unusually successful in every way despite all of the odds. They checked IQs and many socio-economic factors, but they could not come up with a common pattern.

Finally, they decided to interview the successful individuals. As they did, they found only one common theme; they all mentioned the name of the same teacher.

Thinking that this teacher may hold the key to some mystery that could turn the education world on its head, the researchers began to look for her. As it turned out she was no longer a teacher. She only taught for a few years before leaving the profession. In fact, when they went through her records they discovered subpar performance reviews.

But seeing as how she produced so many successful individuals, the researchers persisted in getting an interview with her. They barraged her with questions. Again, nothing seemed to stand out. She wasn't even passionate about the teaching profession.

Finally, as the researchers were about to leave they discovered her secret and the secret of the success of her pupils.

As the researchers were opening the door to exit she said, "Thank you for stopping by. I almost forgot how much I loved those kids."

It was not *what* she did. It was *how* she did it that made all of the difference. Because she loved, she changed the lives of many children. She didn't even know the effect it had, because she wasn't loving them to produce a certain result. She was loving them simply because she loved them.

Loving someone with no strings attached is the greatest gift we can give. It was also the greatest gift given to us by Jesus. Salvation is a free gift with no strings attached.

23

This week I decided to surprise your children with some tests. They were not tests in the traditional sense, because the participants were unaware that they were happening.

My secret tests were actually an examination of character. Would the children pick up garbage that I put in their paths, and thereby demonstrate good stewardship of the pool? Would they put away extra equipment that I purposely left out to help a teammate who may have forgotten? How would the children behave when given less structure, or when it appeared that Coach was occupied with something else?

The results were disappointing. On the behavior test, I would give the children a passing grade, but certainly not an "excellent." The other two tests resulted in a failing grade.

I spoke to the swimmers about the test results, and they responded as I would have expected. They were determined to do the right thing in the future, and were a little sad at the missed opportunity to stand out and be excellent. The most interesting revelation was that EVERY group brought up the same excuse. Every group said they would have done better, if they had only KNOWN it was a test.

To this, I responded that it is ALWAYS the right time to do the right thing. If we only do what is right when we believe others are watching us, then we are hypocrites, with questionable character. Character is what we do when nobody is watching and when nobody notices the results.

Why should we change our behavior when we think it is a test? After all, almost all the important tests we face in our lives are "pop quizzes," which come without warning. We have to have a habit of character, otherwise it isn't character. Would you respond differently to a homeless person if you knew CNN was filming it for an expose? Would you drive 20 mph over the speed limit if you knew there was a State Trooper nearby? Would you visit different websites if your children were in the room with you?

It is easy to demonstrate morality when you know it is a test. But how do you react when you don't know? What matters most is how we respond to circumstances when we aren't being watched, and when we won't get the fanfare. THAT person is who we really are.

Life is full of unexpected opportunities to demonstrate character *if* we pay attention.

WORLDVIEW PART ONE

24

As many of you know, my wife and I did a marathon last Saturday. Without going into it too much, the experience was not a very pleasurable one. Besides just the test of running 26.2 miles, I had issues with cramping legs and a mild tear in my calf muscle.

After only 6 miles of running my goals changed drastically, from hitting a certain time, to merely finishing. When the goal of finishing became too much to bear, I made goals like "run 500 steps." When 500 steps became unbearable it became 100 steps. There were points when 100 steps seemed insurmountable.

Yet, I can honestly say (especially now in hindsight), that even though I suffered immensely and was nowhere near my original goals, the experience was quite enjoyable.

I was reflected a lot this week on the difference between pleasure and enjoyment. Enjoyable things can be pleasurable, but it certainly isn't a requirement. All too often we pursue pleasure, and yet it adds no meaning or value to our lives. On the other hand, those things that are most enjoyable and bring the greatest growth and happiness only happen when we are tested, face some sort of challenge, or exert ourselves in new ways physically or mentally.

Here is another way to think about it. Watching television is pleasurable, but we are not going to tell our grandchildren about "Oh, there was this one time I sat on this couch, and it was so cushy, and this show was on, and I watched the whole thing." At the same time, we will tell the same story 100 times if it added value to our lives and was enjoyable (We'll tell it even more times if it wasn't pleasurable).

As your children continue swimming this season they are bound to face many unpleasurable moments. Holding focus for a long time is typically not pleasurable, swimming 5x200 of anything is not pleasurable, completing "The Josh" or a "Wildcat" is not pleasurable. But, when done well and with correct effort, they are enjoyable because challenges are overcome, there is personal growth, and there is group bonding.

Beware of mistaking pleasure for enjoyment.

25

It is hard to believe that we are already gearing up for the championship portion of the season. Whether your child is a new swimmer, or one trying to make it to Speedo Sectionals, I hope they have enjoyed their time.

While we have a place for everybody on Orcas, as I continue to get to know your children and watch them develop, I have to ask myself "Why is child A talking about school records and Olympic trials and child B still struggling to do X correctly?" This question is especially significant if child A and child B are the same age and have been around for about the same amount of time.

Certain factors are obvious: Child A may come to 6 practices per week while child B comes to 2 on a good week (after all it takes between 7,000 and 10,000 hours of practice at something to become an expert – that's up to 27 years if you practice an hour every day!). Child A may have developed to be 6 feet tall and solid muscle while child B may not have those genetics. Child A may want to be the world's next Michael Phelps, and child B may be content with how things are. (I'm not saying this is wrong by the way, it just produces a different result.)

But then there are those times when it isn't quite so obvious, and it is these athletes over which I spend much time pondering. On the surface, the swimmers appear almost identical. Over time, I have noticed five things about those who ultimately become great and reach their potential.

1) The one who becomes great is always tweaking their skills and learning something new each time they get into the pool. They find ways to make workouts more challenging, and they keep their minds engaged. It is not

the coach doing it; it is the athlete doing it himself. If an athlete says to me, "I'm bored," then they are not engaged like a champion.

2) The one who becomes great is honest in giving and receiving feedback. They don't believe they are perfect. In fact there is a sort of "bold humility" in what they do. They ask the coaches how they can get better, and they bug us if it doesn't feel quite right. They also are honest with themselves when they don't do something like they should, or when they don't put forth the necessary effort. These are the kids who tell me what happened in their race instead of me telling them. Finally, they make changes as a result of that feedback. They don't do the same thing next time and expect a different result.

3) The one who becomes great does things even when it is not fun. Sometime I see kids mentally "check out" as soon as they hear the next set. They don't want to swim 200's with flip turns. They don't want to streamline past the flags when they are tired. They don't want to push themselves after 90 minutes of swimming, etc. Getting better isn't always fun. That's a fact of life. People who are great deal with it.

4) The one who becomes great always looks for areas where he can improve. Then, he tries to get better. If he feels his flip turns are weak, he practices them. This may seem obvious, but a majority of people take the attitude "My flip turns aren't good, so I won't do them." Champions seems to enjoy the discovery that "I'm not good at X," because they see it as opportunity instead of discouragement.

5) The one who becomes great remembers the details and is focused on them in the moment. There is nothing more frustrating to a coach than spending a great deal of time working with someone on something, and then they forget it as soon as you move on to something else. Champions not only remember, but they remember at the right time – while they are doing it! At this point in the season I will often ask the group for some things that we need to remember about technique X. The group will often recite 99% of everything I have told them, but most don't do it because they are not in the moment. So later when I ask, "Why didn't you streamline?" they usually say, "I forgot." To me, "I forgot" usually means "I was thinking about something else." When a champion is streamlining, all their focus is on the streamline.

Now, think about how these five principles also apply to school, to raising a family, and to a career.

Finally, you do not need to define "great" or a "champion" as the person who wins the blue ribbon. These five attitudes help people to be the best THEY can be. It helps each child maximize THEIR potential. This is what we value as a team, even if that child never stands on top of a podium.

26

One neat aspect of your children's hard work and dedication is the fact that the foundation of aerobic fitness set now will carry over for the rest of their life (non-aerobic sports can't do this). But, the most important aspect is that the commitment and dedication they learn in the pool will carry over into the rest of their lives.

Sports are valuable in the sense that they are controlled environments in which children can learn how to deal with things like pain, loss, disappointment, overwhelming obstacles, crammed schedules, having to perform while sick or tired, etc. Life, however, is uncontrolled. When situations come up that produce negatives, children who have already experienced them in a safe sports environment can use what they've learned and handle it in a positive way.

I believe this is one reason why athletes tend to have more success in life than non-athletes. They have had a chance to experience life in a controlled setting.

Now that we've talked about the disappointing things, what about the successes? It may seem strange that I'm worried about how children handle success, but I see them fail more in their successes than in their victories.

How? First, most forget to give the glory to their Creator. Of course, you don't have to say "To God be the glory" to do it. If you feel prideful, then you are giving glory to yourself, not to God. Great victory should feel humbling. Second, many forget the "little people" that got them there. Third, people often abandon what made them successful in the first place. I always shake my head when someone who has worked hard with a certain coach for a number of years switches to another program as soon as they become successful. They have abandoned their team and the reason they got successful to begin with! For some reason, they think that by changing things they will get better. They also forget the importance of giving back to their program.

Sports are a great microcosm of life. But sports won't teach us anything unless we deliberately use it to develop character in both the bad times and the good.

27

I have been thinking again about "talent." It is a little technical, but if you spend some time with it, a whole host of things, even outside of the pool, will become very clear.

I have often wondered why I frequently type the word "the" as "teh." As you probably would guess, I have also often wondered how certain people attain a world class level of ability in our sport, or any sport, for that matter. This week I discovered that the answer to both questions might be the same.

According to "The Cambridge Handbook of Expertise and Expert Performance," a 901-page summary of the latest findings in neurobiology, and in studying phenoms of various pursuits, it all boiled down to myelin. Myelin is a material that covers our neurons, which are the cells that make up nerves. To put it simply, God made our body with a very complex series of nerve pathways. The more a pathway is used, the more myelin is wrapped around each neuron. Myelin is to a nerve, as insulation is to an electric wire. The more myelin, the faster and more accurate a signal passes through our nervous system.

To put it even more simply, "Practice doesn't make perfect, perfect practice makes perfect." Every skill set is a circuit, and that circuit has to be formed and optimized. If you train well, the circuitry is optimized because myelin will become thickest in the pathway that allows a skill to be performed correctly.

What do good athletes do when they train? According to George Bartzokis, Neurology Professor at UCLA, "They send precise impulses along wires that give the signal to myelinate that wire. They end up, after all the training, with a super duper wire – lots of bandwidth, a high speed T-1 line. That's what makes them (world class athletes) different from the rest of us."

I can type over 90 words per minute. But, due to lots of incorrect practice, I've myelinated a pathway that types "the" as "teh." And every time I type it that way, I reinforce that neural circuitry. Michael Phelps swims so fast because he has wired himself to always perform strokes correctly and with a lot of force.

This ties in well with one of the other great books I read last year on talent development, "Mindset" by Carol Dweck. She believes that by focusing on putting effort into the right areas, we produce talent. (That you are born with a talent is a myth, we are born with potential.)

This is just like the results of the Cambridge Handbook. How do they say you produce talent? *Deliberate Practice.* This is defined as "individuals engaging in a practice activity with full concentration on improving some aspect of their performance." You need to stretch yourself into an uncomfortable area beyond what you can quite do. When done correctly, the focus is so great that it is difficult to do for extended periods of time.

So for me, I need to put effort and concentration back into typing, especially with "the." For your children, it means they must focus on doing something correct in the pool every time they do it. Otherwise all neural pathways become equal and no one pathway is dominant and so they become just as likely to not streamline, for instance, as streamline. Hence, no good habit forms.

One last example to help clarify: If I want to get good at hammering a nail, I can't just haphazardly pound away. I need to deliberately concentrate on hitting the head of the nail, otherwise, I don't improve. The more I practice deliberately, the better I will become. If I don't focus on hitting the nail, I may become better at pounding through increased strength, and improve in the sense that I'm stronger for those moments when I actually connect, but I haven't improved in the specific skill of pounding in a nail.

So, the bottom line is, in order to maximize your God-given potential, you need to practice on purpose by devoting conscious attention to an area you want to improve.

28

Last week I did an object lesson with the children that attended morning practice. I brought in donuts (something I do every once in a blue moon for those dedicated enough to swim before school), and told the kids we were going to play a game.

The children were divided into three teams. They were told they had to find their respective note and do what the note said within five minutes to get their treat. The first group's note was in the bleachers – only there was no note, so they just wandered around for a while. The second group's note asked them to balance some tennis balls on top of each other – an impossible task, though they sincerely worked very hard at it. The third group's note simply said that the donuts were a free gift that they could enjoy.

Related to swimming, the first group represented athletes without goals. They come in and are busy wandering around, but they never get any sort of reward. The second group represents those athletes who may have goals that are too lofty or those who want to do things their own way. They work really hard (or not) and never get what they want. The third group represents those who listen to their coach and seize the opportunity to learn from those here to help them. By doing what they're told, they'll reach their goals. Obviously, this is the easiest route.

There is a much broader object lesson that can be learned from this related to Christmas. Even though the Bible has been repeatedly proven to be more historically accurate than any other history book prior to the invention of the printing press, and even though it has changed countless lives despite persecution and the attempts of many to destroy or discredit it, many people still reject it. Countless others have never even heard of it. This is represented by the first group wandering around aimlessly. They try this and that to gain happiness, but wind up disappointed, or they turn to escape and bitterness. They may turn to false religions (even those proven to be false!) because something inside of them longs for the eternal, but they never find peace.

Many others may read the Bible or go to church and even profess Jesus, but they still believe they can earn their way into heaven. They believe they must "do things for God" or that their good deeds must outweigh their bad deeds. This, of course, is impossible when you realize the standard is to "be perfect as your Father in heaven is perfect." These people are represented by the second swim group. We all have told lies and been unloving towards others, and let's not even get into our thoughts, where the standard is that they MUST be pure at all times.

The final group is those that cling to the free gift promised throughout the New Testament and predicted throughout the Old Testament. "For by grace you have been saved through faith. And this is not your own doing; it is the gift of Got not a result of works so that no one may boast." Ephesians 2:8-9.

This is the message and true meaning of Christmas. Christmas wouldn't be good news if all paths lead to the same place (Why then did Jesus come and die?). It wouldn't be good news if you had to endure the impossible task of earning your way into heaven. It can only be good news if you accept the free gift so that as Jesus says, "Whoever believes in me, though he die, yet shall he live."

29

At the beginning of the season I mentioned that, when push comes to shove, "Who really cares how fast someone can swim from point A to point B?" Honestly, it's pretty silly and somewhat shallow to base our identity on how fast we can swim. And it is funny to think that we may swim a few miles at practice, but in the end we haven't really travelled anywhere.

Plus, the truth is, though it is fun to reminisce about "glory days," I don't have any medals or trophies or ribbons on display at my house – I think they're all in a box somewhere at my parent's house. Now that I'm older, I realize they aren't very important.

BUT, what is important is what happens to your sons and daughters as they develop into swimmers (I won't mention how it has also developed me as a parent of a swimmer). It is the journey to those medals, and the striving to go as fast as they can that builds your child's character and develops them into young ladies and gentlemen. It is the good habits they learn that will carry them through life. Habits, like holding themselves to high standards of excellence with the desire to succeed even when it is hard, will determine how we react to life. It is also about the healthy lifestyle they absorb. It is about learning to be a part of a team – having patience and relating to people who are very different from you.

We all need to remember that a team is more than just a group of individuals. A team is an organism whose participants, working together in pursuit of a single goal, achieve far greater success as a whole than would any of its parts working alone or in smaller groups. Each team member has a contribution to make, and from greatest to least, all are equally important. This comes from knowing that others (even those on different teams) work just as hard as you and deserve respect.

Being on a team is about character, integrity, and even time management. It is about developing a healthy competitive nature, powerful work ethic, and fearlessness in meeting the challenges of life. It is about knowing how to fail and how to be gracious in success. It is about building up others when they are down, and about humbling themselves and allowing others to build them up when they are down.

Part of being on a team is knowing that hard work and dedication are never wasted, for though we can't always be the leader or take first place or be the best, we can all make a positive difference in someone's life.

So, after many miles of swimming, your sons and daughters may not have travelled anywhere, but they have certainly gone some place.

30

This week I started to think of how we all, whether in swimming or otherwise, wish to be great. "Great" is a relative term, but regardless of how you define it, you will probably agree that very few get the opportunity to spontaneously do something that would classify their life as great.

For the rest of us, we have to build up our bank account, figuratively speaking, before something great can be produced. To continue the analogy, it may take one million dollars of output before a life is great. Some, like a 9/11 firefighter, may have earned that all at once. For most of us, however, it comes by depositing 50 cents here and a couple of dollars there – in the form of a kind word here and a helping hand there. But a million dollars is a million dollars, and that makes for no less greatness.

This is true of people we would consider to be great swimmers. Mark Spitz or Michael Phelps did not become great in their 20 second or two minute races. They were great before that point, but few knew of their swimming greatness before the races that made them famous. In fact, it was the many hours in the pool making 50 cent deposits that led to their greatness – working hard on technique, waking up early when everyone else was in bed, and pushing themselves, when all they wanted to do was quit.

But there are countless other swimmers who put in the same amount of effort who didn't gain fame, and their swimming greatness is no less. In fact, fame and fortune tend to distract from greatness instead of adding to it – especially when they are the goal instead of the effect.

As we begin this week, I want to encourage you as parents to help your children become great. A great swimmer is nice, but a great person is of much more value. However, much of what we learn on our team – Spirit, Sportsmanship, Dedication, Motivation, and Excellence – will help your sons and daughters with greatness in all aspects of their life. That is the goal of Orcas.

31

I just wanted to take a moment to again thank you for the opportunity to work with your children. Our children are certainly a blessing and a reward! Honestly, there are times when I sit back and am just in awe of the fact that I have been given this wonderful gift – the chance to work with your children. I think it is important for coaches, teachers, and everyone who works with children, to occasionally recognize the fact that you, as parents, are sharing your blessing with us. What an awesome and humbling responsibility, and I thank you for trusting me and the rest of the Orca family with it.

I also want to use this moment as a reminder that your children will not be around forever. They are going to grow up and move away. Likely, they will start families of their own. You only get approximately 18 years with them before they move on. Though it may seem like a long time, it will go by quickly. You will wish you had spent more time with them.

Though we are grateful for the opportunity to work with your children, I pray that it will never be at the expense of you, the parents, spending quality time with them. They need your time. You can't get it back.

32

Last week was one of those weeks that make a coach proud. Your children completed some workouts that require a lot of courage, mental toughness, and good ole' fashioned guts. One girl said to me during a particularly hard session, "Coach, my stomach hurts." And then she kept right on swimming, as if it were a comment rather than a complaint.

In our sport, there is a principle called "the overload principle." Essentially, an athlete works really hard, then their body recovers so that it can be worked harder the next time. On top of becoming stronger physically, this principle teaches young athletes that they can give more than they ever thought possible. They are stronger than they think. They are mentally tougher than they think. They are capable of more than they ever realized. We hope this knowledge helps them in all areas of life.

What makes my heart even more glad is when I see your children willing to push themselves even harder than we coaches push them – especially when it is for the benefit of others. At the charity event on Saturday, I saw some amazing things from your children. I saw a five-year-old who could barely get across the pool a month ago, swim nearly a mile, and an 11 year old swim 4 ½ miles! Every single swimmer there swam more than I would have imagined.

I saw children with burn marks, from their swim suits rubbing, decide that it was worth the pain to raise an extra couple of dollars for people with cancer. I saw children who were cold and tired and sore decide to keep going – even after they were told that it was okay to quit - in order to help someone else. That is the core of the Orca Way. You should be very proud of your children.

33

Let me begin by passing along a belated "Happy Mother's Day" to all of our Orca moms. We truly appreciate all that you do for your children, including making sacrifices so that your children can swim on our team. We hope and believe that "the Orca Way" will make a positive difference in your child's life.

I am reminded of the final line of Laura Ingalls Wilder's book, "Little House in the Big Woods," "They could not be forgotten, she thought, because now is now. It can never be a long time ago." As caregivers of children, we come to the realization at some point that "the days are long, but the years are short," and that today becomes a long time ago too quickly. All of those moments that we invest in (or ignore) our children are slowly forming and shaping and molding them into the next generation. And they will use the influence you had on them to form the next, and they the next, etc.

Yet, sometimes we may undervalue the moments we have with them, not realizing that we are shaping the world of tomorrow – today! I have never met a person who has regretted the time they spent with their children. But sadly, I have met some who regret that they were so busy preparing for "the future" that they neglected the present – thinking that somehow material gifts for their children are the best things they can offer.

When I was a lifeguard in Chicago at a "well-to-do" country club, there were far too many times when a young child would come up to me and say, "I wish you were my dad." I sincerely believe that this was because their parents were making the sort of investments they would later come to regret. I want to encourage you to continue to invest in the moments you have with your children, as they will return the largest dividends in the future.

34

Recently, I attended swimming coach clinic. I would like to thank the parent's board (and by extension all of you) for allowing me to participate and further refine my skills under the guidance of Olympic Coaches, International level coaches, and world record holding athletes.

A couple of things that struck me that I would like to share with all of you. First of all, and this may seem obvious, all of these "great" coaches and athletes are no different from you and me. I was in the elevator with a former Olympic Coach and saw him struggle with his luggage. I saw a world record holder in the hotel pool, who should have been told to pull up his trunks a bit. I mention these because they are very ordinary (and somewhat embarrassing) things that we all do.

The second thing I noticed is that they, though ordinary people, have done and are doing extraordinary things. In watching how the coaches and athletes worked together, and in hearing many great talks, I realized that what they have done is very simple in concept but somewhat harder in reality.

Let's look at an athlete. An athlete doesn't just one day break a world record. Once upon a time, if you threw this world record holder into the pool, he would have drowned. He simply got a little better every single day.

Try this sometime. Take a stopwatch. Start and stop it as fast as you can. This is a game I often play with the kids. You can do this in roughly 1/10 of a second. I would be willing to bet that most of your children believe that they can improve their 50 freestyle by that much in a week. If they did that every week for a year, they would be 5 seconds faster! What if they did that every day? I bet most of your children have about five or ten things that they "know" they could do to make their 50 freestyle that much better right now! This is how you do something extraordinary – improve 1/10 of a second at a time.

The third and final thing that I will share with you is that we are ALL capable of getting 1/10 of a second better – as parents, in our jobs, in respecting one another, etc. But the key to excellence is not to get 1/10 of a second better here and lose 1/2 of a second there. We can't forget the lessons of the past!

I truly believe that our children are capable of doing some amazing things, in and out of the pool, if we all remember "the rule of 1/10".

35

On this Memorial Day, I would like to reflect a little bit on the Orca Way value of "Spirit". It may seem odd to some that a swim coach would be tying together the team's values with Memorial Day (aside from the fact that I'm a current member of the Armed Forces). However, as Mark Schubert (7-time USA Olympic Coach) stated, "You don't have to do much international travel to realize how lucky we are, and our children need to learn at an early age how trivial most of our major concerns are." I think this is especially true in a city as blessed as Waunakee.

Most of you don't know that my wife, Reka, grew up in Communist Romania. The stories her family tells seem so foreign as to almost be fanciful. They told me about heat being turned off in the middle of winter, property seized for no reason, and relatives being thrown in jail for years without any trial or even letting someone else know. They mentioned how husbands and wives were not allowed to vacation at the same time, having to bring your own sheets to the hospital if you wanted clean ones, sharing a hospital bed with another while giving birth, and police beating people in the streets. Reka's family knew of children being taken from their "traitorous" parents, standing in lines and not knowing why because whatever is at the end of that line is probably something you need, and of private phones being "bugged." They felt hopelessness, hunger, and humiliation at the hands of their government. The list could go on and on.

Believe it or not, one of the first things my wife's family did, when they came to America, was take pictures of the inside of a grocery store, because they were shocked at our abundance!

I have personally known people from Switzerland, Germany, England, Italy, France, Palestine, Iceland, India, China, Japan, Korea, Indonesia, Rwanda, South Africa, Chile, Argentina, Jamaica, and more. All have challenged me to acknowledge how fortunate we are to live in the United States. I have heard even more stories from my military "brothers and sisters" about how other people across the world live - and how they envy us (some to the point of hatred).

I hope you will make it a point to let your child know how lucky we are to live in a place where the most common concern I see is whether or not our pool is 82 degrees or 84 degrees. So please, remind your children that we are not entitled to such luxury, that it is earned – and often at a very high price. And when you realize that price, you are filled with humility and responsibility knowing that people have died for you, and their families suffered for you, when there was nothing you did to deserve it.

36

Over the next few weeks our coaching theme will be: "Spend time on things that are profitable." By profitable I mean "that which is good and useful – those things which will yield advantageous results."

It seems obvious. Why would you waste your time on things that, well . . . waste your time? But we all do it. We worry about things that never happen, trade our life for a couple of extra bucks, humor our bad habits, etc. The reality is that we don't need to be enslaved to these things.

For instance, did you know that if the average person stopped watching television for a year and used that time instead for reading, they could read a book the size of the Bible 20 times, and still have enough time left over to prepare for and run a marathon? Sometimes we just need to sit back and ask ourselves, "Is what I'm doing to myself really worth my time or am I better than that?" Bad habits must be replaced.

In swimming this mentality becomes "If I have to be in this swimming pool for an hour, I might as well use it to get better. I should use this time to streamline or keep my head down or elbows up or kick like I really mean it. By the end of the season, those things that I struggle with now could be a habit that makes me more like the swimmer I want to become".

I would like to challenge everyone to think about where they want to be at the end of the season and then, "Carpe Diem!"

37

I told the children that the way to a successful year of swimming is to put together a few successful months. The way to a successful month is to have a few successful weeks. The way to a successful week is to have a few successful days. The way to a day is to have a few successful sets. The way to have a successful set is having a few successful moments.

This is true of life as well – whether in starting a company, losing weight, or deciding to do a triathlon for the first time. When you read about successful people from all walks of life, they seem to have a couple of things in common.

The first thing they do well is set appropriate goals to pursue. Then, they work backwards from that goal to see where they need to be at different points in time. Next, they break that down into a plan. Finally, they follow through with that plan, knowing that in every choice they make they are either setting themselves up for success or failure.

Like water dripping from a cave, the seemingly insignificant can produce dramatic effects over time.

38

Many ancient books of wisdom, including the Bible, use vessel imagery to symbolize humanity. Like a glass or a cup, we cannot pour anything out that has not been put in. And though we cannot fill a container above the top, it is always best to maximize potential. I shared this symbol with your children last week, because it is quite apt for swimming.

We also carried this imagery further. I brought in a two liter bottle for each of the five groups, and explained, "When you fill your cup, you are contributing to the team and helping everyone else reach their potential." To symbolize this, every time a child has a good practice, they get to put one capful of water into the two-liter bottle. Though one capful is not very much, all of our efforts together add up to big things.

But then I wondered, "What do I even mean when I say "big things?"" It is true that coming to more practices means your children will improve more, and that means we will do better at meets as a team, and then maybe other teams around the state will (and have already) tell us how impressed they are with such a young organization. Ok, that's fine . . . but ultimately, so what?

This week I heard the story of Steve Jobs. Now, most of you know quite a bit about the president of Apple. What this man did *literally changed the world*. Our planet will never be the same because of his inventions and ideas. This seems like the type of "big thing" that anyone would want for themselves and their organization.

But, there is another story about Steve Jobs. Even with his successes, even though he changed the world, and even though he has donated millions to various charities, it is rumored that he has left in his wake many destroyed lives. Though his actions seem like big things, his character allegedly has left him despised by nearly everyone he knows. Though he did what he loved, it seems love is something he lacks. In my opinion, if this is true (and I hope that it is not or even if it were, that it has changed), then Mr. Jobs has accomplished absolutely nothing in his life.

In swimming, we can't control who will be the next state or national or Olympic champion. Perhaps an athlete's swimming cup can only be filled to the level of someone relatively mediocre. But we can control how we treat our teammates, our opponents, and our community. By focusing on our values of Spirit, Sportsmanship, Dedication, Motivation, and Excellence, we can do big things from the heart. And that is truly accomplishing something.

39

I mentioned to your children last Monday what many philosophers have called "the paradox of hedonism." That is, you cannot find happiness by seeking it. In fact, nothing will lead to despair more quickly than seeking your own happiness.

It doesn't take much thought to realize the truth of this paradox. If your sole evaluation of everything is "how does it make me feel," then everything becomes a means to an empty and selfish end . . . including our own children! It seems we are wired for more than just happiness, and certainly for more than just seeking it. Case in point is what happens to most celebrities versus Mother Theresa.

Even the Declaration of Independence mentions that everyone has an inalienable right to pursue happiness, but what most people don't realize is that the definition of happiness has changed a lot in the last 80 years. Happiness, in the classical sense, means pursuing virtue, wisdom, meaningful relationships, and being a part of some greater purpose. It is nearly the opposite of how we tend to define it today!

In swimming, this is certainly true. We can have joy by suffering through a workout, knowing that we are a part of something larger (the team), creating relationships with peers while avoiding trouble, and obtaining character attributes like perseverance and discipline. We are able to take what we started in the pool and use that to make Orcas a part of something even larger, the community. We do this by participating in Special Olympics, Autism Speaks, Relay for Life, Operation Christmas Child, Waunakee Food Pantry, and benefits for children living in our community. Trophies, medals, and state-cut times are nice, but it is in giving of ourselves to something larger that we produce the most real and lasting joy.

As adults, it is important that we not forget this truth as well.

40

Watching the state meet this weekend made me think about how we have two choices in our lives. We can choose to be a celebrity or we can choose to be a hero. (I guess there is a third choice, which is to be in isolation. However, most only pursue it for a short period of time so it requires no further explanation.) Let's look at the differences between being a celebrity and being a hero.

A celebrity is one who is individualistic. Not that individualism is bad, but once you go too far with it, it is destructive, as in the case of a celebrity who does his own thing and seeks to create meaning by looking within his own self. A celebrity is infantile, seeking instant gratification, comfort, and soothing. This person is controlled by cravings and constantly seeks to fill himself with things likes food, lust, image, entertainment, material goods, etc. A celebrity is narcissistic. They manipulate others to validate their self-esteem. They are preoccupied with self-interest – education enhances career, children make me look good (if they are selfless enough to even have children), exercise makes me look good and helps me to win, my spouse fulfills my needs and should worship me, etc. A celebrity is passive. They let other people do their thinking and living for them—even if it is a false self-portrayed to the world. They are in search of pleasure and consumer goods provided by others. They expect others to sacrifice for them. The bottom line is that a celebrity is dependent on external circumstances and individuals to find any sense of worth.

A hero is someone who is bound by duty, virtue, and community. They see themselves as a part of something larger and greater than their individual life. Meaning comes from doing the right thing, at the right time, especially when they are not going to get any glory. The hero accepts pain, suffering, and discipline as a part of growing and giving of themselves for the greater good. There is a more long term approach to everything. Happiness is not sought after, but it is the result of their living for others. Others are not a means to a selfish end, but rather a means to a selfless end—another chance to give. A hero is active. They know that the little things in life are truly dramatic in the struggle to live a life of wisdom, virtue, kindness, goodness, and character. They realize that even the ordinary is a part of the grand struggle against darkness, so the little things become big and extraordinary very quickly. The bottom line is that a hero finds that they can only obtain happiness from within, and they care not for a fleeting amount of pleasurable satisfaction, because it is not the point and not even worth worrying about.

Clearly, a hero can become a celebrity—in the sense of one who is well known. But their celebrity status is based on something real and tangible, the opposite of how most celebrities become known. But in swimming, as in life, a hero often is the one who doesn't make it to the state meet and doesn't win the races. Instead, they push others to their greatness. They are a part of the community, of the team, and realize that their role is support and personal bests. They may never get the gold medal, but they enjoy themselves nevertheless, because of what is gained in the process— discipline, patience, endurance, learning how to win and lose, character, cooperation, sacrifice for another, sacrifice for a greater good, friendships, learning how to push themselves beyond what they thought capable, etc.

A celebrity can almost never become a true hero so long as they pursue being a celebrity. They may do things associated with heroism, but with the purpose of advancing celebrity status. Or they may do things out of guilt, but not to the point where real suffering is involved. They play it cool and act like they don't care, because to care means to be emotionally involved.

A hero will be pleased with themselves no matter the outcome, if they have done all they could up to this point. They will resolve to do better if they have knowingly failed in their duties and did not get the desired outcome. A celebrity will be gracious with themselves no matter the outcome. If the outcome is not what they like, they will blame others or quit, never taking personal responsibility for their life.

We all have two choices. One leads to true happiness. The other leads to a sense of busyness without any fulfillment.

41

Quick! Answer this riddle: Three frogs are on a lily pad. One decides to jump in. How many are left on the lily pad? I hope that each of you answered correctly. Three. Deciding and actually doing something are very different things. It seems that great ideas are a dime a dozen, but those who act on those ideas are scarce.

Whether it is simply to devote yourself to exercise or to start your own business, we tend to admire individuals with follow-through. Why? Because it is rare. Some get paralyzed by analysis. Others fear failure. Others simply are lazy or are not devoted to improvement. It is never too late to act upon good ideas. The time is always right to do the right thing. Now is a great time to teach your children the value of putting in effort and not just wishing for good things to come true. The best way for us to help them is to demonstrate this characteristic ourselves!

This past week the children decided to swim well at our first meet at a 50-meter pool (A 50-meter pool is same type of pool in which the Olympics and other international level competitions are held). Then, they acted upon it.

As a team, we also decided to help benefit cancer research and show our support to those who have fought the good fight against cancer. This decision was acted upon by walking together at Relay for Life. I am very proud of your children for both accomplishments.

Yet we still have many areas where, with some effort, we can improve as a team and as individuals. As a coach, it is my job to spot those areas so that we can work on them, as we will this week. As a parent, it is your job to know your child's ambitions and to make sure their actions reflect their desires. It is both my job and your job to make sure those desires are appropriate. I love the idea of all of us working together to help your children reach their potential.

42

I think our White group children learned a valuable lesson about the importance of teamwork this past week. We were doing a kicking set and I told them if any swimmer hit a certain time, the whole group would be done. Instead of each person giving their best, the group expected the best kicker to do it on his own. He missed the time by about 3 seconds.

What they realized was that while Person A may be the fastest, they can't do their best unless the second fastest, Person B, is chasing them. Person B can't do her best unless Person C is giving 100% to catch her. And so forth, all the way down the line. John Maxwell said, "The belief that one person can do something great is a myth. Nothing great ever happened without a team."

This leads to two additional lessons that are also true in life: 1) We need to realize that we are not the savior of our little part of the world. 2) Our role is essential, no matter how seemingly insignificant we may feel. In other words we shouldn't feel too good about ourselves, nor should we feel too bad about ourselves. But we should be very pleased with *us*, and the freedom and relief that comes from being part of a team.

Being part of a team will propel us to maximize our potential without burdensome pressure or feelings of inadequacy or insecurity.

43

I got to thinking a little bit about what actually makes a team "a team" and not "a group." Many people use the terms interchangeably, but I believe there are some fundamental differences.

1) Groups are easy to form. Teams are not. When you signed your child up for Orcas, initially, all you did was add them to a group, and what you probably thought was "I hope this helps my child get what they need." Then we took this group of kids and divided them into different smaller practice groups. Then I took that practice group and divided it down even further into a group that swims in lane 5, a group in lane 6, a group in lane 7, etc. In a team, each member must have a function or a purpose. In other words, each child must have something to GIVE and they must have a sense of what that something is. A team's overall success depends upon how well each individual member performs at giving. In athletics, it is not always easy to find that purpose in the early going. It is easy to look at an athlete atop the podium and know their purpose, but what does a 4-year-old child give to the team? (I have an answer for that, but I will leave it rhetorical). What can the child in lane 8 give to others in lane 8? What can she give to the person in lane 7? What can she give to the group above and below her? What is her job in this race at this specific moment in time?

2) Groups measure success in final results. Teams worry more about the process and let the final results be what they may. A great example of a group is a trial jury where consensus is the goal. "We have a verdict; hence, we are a success." Unfortunately, many so-called teams also proudly display this mentality – "We took X place at state," is so common that it is often unnoticed. But that is merely letting circumstances beyond your control determine your worth. We can't control what the team in the next

town over is doing or what their genetics are or if a flu bug went through or anything else that happens outside our walls (and probably less than 50% of what happens within our walls!). By focusing on the process and controlling what can be controlled, we will improve. By constantly looking to our values, we will succeed.

3) Groups train people. Teams develop people. I'm sure you see the subtlety here, but let me add: In a group, the leader sees people as a reflection of who they are. In other words, there is a lot of pride involved. "If they do well, then I am great. If they fail, I am upset with them, because they make me look like a failure." In a group, the instructions are often "Do X, Y, and Z or you're out" or "you will always do A because you are our A." On a team, there is freedom to explore and make mistakes. The leadership recognizes there is a life outside of the leader's personal ambitions, and that sometimes it is better for the member to go a different route.

4) In a group, members are insecure. On a team, members have a healthy self-esteem based on growth and maturity. In a group, we are always trying to prove ourselves as if the competition is the person next to us. "I can't let them look better than me." There is a lot of putting others down to build yourself up. On a team, you only truly compete against one person – yourself. But that competition is about achieving excellence and doing so, at least partially, for that person next to us. This creates self-esteem and a bond with another person that isn't easily broken.

I suppose I could go on and on with this, but let me just say that our goal in Orcas is to concentrate on developing a *team*. Again, our motto this season is "Every swimmer. Every race. Every time." As parents, you influence your child more than anyone else, and I know you will help us try to achieve this goal of developing a team. Help your child realize what they can give to the team and what their purpose is or might be. Help your child see that *how* things are done is just as important as *what* is done. Let your child make mistakes and let them be challenged. Encourage them during this time. Keep your children focused on their improvement and not on what someone else did in comparison.

44

I have been thinking a lot about relationships. It began as I thought about how a team interacts, and how, though we continue to improve, we still have a long way to go to get to the point where those interactions are truly meaningful. This theme continued to snowball in my mind after I watched the movie "Fireproof" (great movie, I recommend it), heard a sermon about it at church, and had some interaction this week with individuals concerned about their relationships.

I came to the conclusion that, for the most part, we are all pretty bad at relationships. Oh, we are great at being polite. And we are great at interacting well at social and surface levels. We are great at reaching out to people when our circle of friends is not complete. But once work begins, the type that requires us to dedicate time or put in additional effort to move to the next level, we resist and become consumed with other things. Below are a small variety of comments I heard this week:

- "Don't interrupt me, I'm watching the game." Since when does it become an interruption to our life to relate to somebody else? Why is our priority to watch some people we don't know play a meaningless game?

- "The conversation was fine, but then they brought up X." Why must our relationships become estranged when others don't affirm us, or disagree with our way of thinking?

- "I don't have time to deal with that person." Perhaps not, but what is so important that another human being takes a back burner?

- "I wish I knew so and so better." Or "I hope that person makes some friends on the team." Why do we become so moral and value relationships so much when we want someone else to do the work? Why is it such a chore to reach out to someone when our current needs are fulfilled?

One of the values we have as a team is dedication. It is fine to be dedicated to many different things, but it should not be at the cost of dedication to one another. I realize that my guilt is no less than any of yours. I speak to your children often, but I seldom interact with most of you.

My hope is that, as a team, we can begin to strengthen our relationships with one another, to take the next step beyond cursory remarks and polite greetings. I want to encourage you to get to know one another better, to step out of your comfort zone when you see a face you don't recognize (after all, you certainly have something in common if you are at the pool together) or to deepen a relationship with someone you know. For example, we all have to eat meals, what a great opportunity! It breaks my heart when the season is half over and I find out that new families still don't know anyone. It is depressing to hear that someone has been on the team for a couple of seasons and is scared to do anything but drop their child off because nobody talks to them in the bleachers.

We could all do a better job of setting the example as to what it means to be dedicated to one another. Our children deserve to see us valuing others.

45

Does it really matter what swim team a child is on, or is it an issue as frivolous as "Do I wear a red shirt or a purple shirt today?"

I'm going to answer that question by sharing with you something special that happened at the regional meet last weekend.

One of our ten-year-olds found $20 lying on the pool deck. He didn't know who it belonged to, so he approached me to ask what he should do with it. I asked the usual question about if he saw someone drop it and, except for one clue, there was no way we could determine the owner. That one clue was that he found it near a camping chair.

We had no idea whose chair it was, but chairs on the pool deck generally belong to volunteers, officials, or coaches (aka "adults"), so I told this swimmer to put the money on the chair and we'd wait and see what happened. In my head I was thinking, "If it is not that person's money we can go to the organizers and see if it gets claimed."

Not even a minute a later, a coach from a different team came our direction and exclaimed, "Hey, someone put some money on my chair!" He then grabbed the money, one ten dollar bill in each hand, and did a joyous little dance, while making some other childish exclamations.

At that point, one of our assistants said, "Our boy found that, and we thought it might be yours, so he put it on your chair. I guess it isn't yours."

The other coach responded that is was not his, and then proceeded to gloat more about how he found $20. At that point, I thought the gleeful dancing *must* be a ruse, whereby he was just trying to be funny. But to be certain, we pointed out again that a young boy on our team found it and was trying to do the right thing.

The other coach then pocketed the money and walked away. I double checked to see if the money was either turned in or, as most adults would do, given to our boy, but it was not. He was not trying to be funny after all.

Regardless of his ability to teach swimming, this coach demonstrated his worldview and the importance of character. His was sold for a lousy twenty bucks. It was such a stark difference between what we teach on Orcas, and what so much of the world around us believes.

Our worldview affects EVERYTHING. And, sadly, there are plenty of people who don't care about character, for the sake of being a part of a team that may score a few extra points.

That said, here are some other tidbits about that team: They generally don't accept an athlete unless she has a certain level of ability for her age. They don't have anyone on their team who is disabled or who has cognitive issues. They recruit from other programs and take the credit for the years of hard work that others have done, often times by slandering those other programs. Their stated goal is winning and they will sacrifice other values (that most of us hold dear) in order to get there. They are constantly in trouble with both Wisconsin Swimming and the facility where they practice because of safety and ethical violations.

Yet, people flock to that program because they are promised (often falsely) one thing that our culture overemphasizes – winning.

That's a HUGE difference in perspective that comes from worldview. My worldview, and the worldview our team was founded on, is Christian. We are not a Christian team, but my Christianity affects all I do as a coach.

There truly is a difference! We created a values-based team so that kids can grow both as athletes and as human beings. Orcas bucked the trend that we see in youth sports today. I hope more teams realize that winning is a far lesser virtue than character development.

46

Recently, I pondered the difference between "loving somebody" and "making much of somebody." Unfortunately, I think there is a lot of confusion between the two. Making much of somebody may be one aspect of loving somebody, but in our culture it gets far too much attention and is sometimes viewed as the only way to love.

The truth is that sometimes making much of others is one of the most unloving things we can do. As a swimming coach, the most unloving thing I can do is assure people they are great just the way they are, and that they don't need to improve. As an athlete, the most deadly thing one can do is to make too much of oneself (this is different from being confident or optimistic). As a parent, letting your child usurp your role by making too much of the child leads to all sorts of mayhem.

I mention this because I often catch glimpses in our culture, and sometimes specifically on our team, where "to be made much of" is the goal. Occasionally, "to be made much of" is presented as if it were a right. Believing that it is a right "to be made much of" or to pursue it as a goal are both very unhealthy and will, ultimately, ruin a team. Energy becomes focused entirely on "how you make me feel," which leads to great insecurity, because then self-esteem is based on others doting over you.

When others don't dote, then gossip, squabbling, and power plays start to break up camaraderie. It also leads to instability because, though everyone is important and everyone truly matters, no one person should be getting all of the attention – nor can they! On the flip side, we all know deep down if we've done something worthy of discipline. If people respond the same way, regardless of our behavior, we know they are not genuine and we can no longer trust their opinion. And for those who have known no other way but to be constantly made much of, they will have a very rude awakening one day.

So what are we to do? The answer is very simple: the best we can. We need to set our own internal standards so that our esteem is rooted in that which we can control. We need to focus our energy on effort and self-improvement. We need to look to those we trust for encouragement, but more importantly, we need to be an encourager.

The best way to get all that you want is to give all that you can. Giving has a strange way of adjusting what we want to get, if done in an altruistic way.

When we have a healthy view of ourselves, not an inflated view, we can focus on others and thus on making our team, our family, and our world a better place.

47

I was thinking a bit about our core values: Spirit, Sportsmanship, Dedication, Motivation, and Excellence. Values are a lot like character – it is not tested during trials and difficulties, it is *revealed* during trials and difficulties.

Spirit is easy when everyone agrees with you. Sportsmanship is a breeze when others are nice to you. Dedication isn't an issue if you don't believe that the grass may be greener elsewhere. Motivation is simple when you are doing something that you want to do. Excellence is always attained if the standard is low enough.

But who we really are, and what we really value comes to light when we are faced with challenges. How is your spirit when you are tired and there is an opportunity to give back? How is your sportsmanship when others treat you unfairly? How is your dedication once the honeymoon is over? How is your motivation when you need to do something that isn't fun, even if you know it will benefit you? What happens to excellence when you give an unbiased look at yourself?

I don't want us to be a team that merely pays lip service to our values. We can justify actions all we want, but it won't change the truth about our character and how we adhere to our values. How we are when others are watching, is how we should be even when they are not watching.

At some point our true values will be revealed, so we shouldn't be surprised when we reap what we have sown.

A Wise Person Once Said . . .

48

Mark Spitz, the great American Swimmer, once said, "They rattle off 20 different reasons why they didn't do something. Almost 100% of the time they were capable of doing exactly what they said they should have done. But they didn't."

At the end of a season, we coaches often start to hear the "coulda, woulda, and shoulda's." The lesson is that, "Yes, you could have, but you didn't." After reminding the athlete of this, the most important thing becomes helping those who regret their actions not make the same mistake in the future.

This is a great time to remind everyone of the brevity of life. It won't be long and the "season" will be over. Did you focus on what you should have or did you ignore the eternal? Did you use the gifts God gave you, or did you squander your talents? Was your only gain selfish or did you make a real difference? Is the world better, is the Kingdom advanced, because you were here?

So instead of worrying about the past – which we can't change and can never get back – coaches try to get athletes to concern themselves with the present time, over which we have control. We learn from the past, but that opportunity is lost.

By looking at the present, we make a difference in both now and the future. The future can be changed by lessons learned from the past as long as you incorporate it into the present!

Every moment you are moping about where you failed in the past, you are ruining a moment in the present and wasting future potential. Unless you are on your death bed, there is always time to change for the better.

49

I was thinking a lot this week about the Orca value "excellence." In particular I have been thinking about how excellence affects a group dynamic. In the Orca Statement of Excellence, which was passed along at the beginning of the season, there is the point, "I will do everything I can to help my teammates pursue excellence."

I think a lot of us understand what this means from the positive side, encouragement, sportsmanship, and the like, but there is another side of helping others pursue excellence. We need to pursue excellence ourselves.

We can't tell others to work hard and then be lazy ourselves. We can't tell others to listen to the coach if we don't listen and learn. We can't encourage others to make practice fun, if we are the ones being disruptive or disrespectful. What we do means a lot more than where we pay lip service.

There is a proverb, "People who accept discipline are on the pathway to life, but those who ignore correction lead others astray." I don't think the meaning of this really hit me until this week. Discipline, in all its forms, is not really a battle *against* ourselves, it is a battle *for* ourselves. When we are disciplined, we train the best parts of ourselves to overcome the parts of ourselves we can do without. This was not a new insight for me. The part I didn't understand was the second half, how ignoring correction not only hurts us, it hurts other people as well.

Let's face it, none of us know everything. We all need correction from time to time. You have trusted teachers and coaches with your children in large part so that we can correct them. When correction is ignored, others believe that their mistakes aren't "that bad" or that the whole thing "must not be that important." It can become a plague to the whole organization until eventually excellence is lost.

We need correction. It is a blessing to ourselves and to others. We should value correction so that we do not continue to make the same mistakes repeatedly, and so that others hopefully don't make them in the first place. Also, one of the most loving thing we can do is correct others in a constructive way. To not correct someone is to give up on them.

So, Orcas, when you are corrected realize that it isn't something negative, and work with diligence so that your correction benefits others as well.

50

I recently heard a great quote from basketball legend Michael Jordan that I wanted to share with all of you: "I've missed more than 9,000 shots in my career. I've lost almost 300 games. Twenty-six times, I've been trusted to take the game winning shot and missed. I've failed over and over and over again in my life. And that is why I succeed."

One of our Orca values is "dedication." Obviously, this is an attribute that Michael Jordan shares with us.

How else could you say that your failures are the reason you succeed? Some things that we hope to teach in Orcas are: You can learn just as much from disappointment as you can from success – probably more. You will not be great at something the first time you try it . . . or the second . . . or maybe the 100th, but if you are dedicated to it, eventually you will be and your success will be all the sweeter. The only time you've really failed is when you've failed to try. Things may seem dark at the present, but what you want may be just around the corner.

And probably the most important: Being dedicated to something is worthless unless you are dedicated to the RIGHT thing, as some thoughts are simply more valid than others . . . in swimming, as in life.

51

I saw a poster the other day that said the following, "At 211 degrees, water is hot. At 212 degrees, it boils. And with boiling water comes steam. And steam can power a locomotive." That one degree makes all the difference. Keep encouraging your children to put in that little extra effort and be proud of them when they do.

Now comes the time in the season when that little bit of extra effort can make a big difference in how well your children swim. At the same time, we will not forget that your children are just that, children. They need opportunities to explore. They need time to play. Frankly, they just need time to be kids! They can't do this if every moment of their time is structured.

We have found that occasionally giving the children "free time" to play in the pool not only helps psychologically, but it actually helps them physically. Often times, they will play harder than they train. They will do things on their own to be more athletic. In short, "free time" can provide the extra heat to add an extra degree.

Don't forget the importance of allowing kids be kids.

52

T. S. Eliot once said, "Only those who risk going too far can possibly find out how far one can go." When you look at some of the greatest athletes in different sports, there is something you may not notice at first because you are awed by their greatness. It is their failures. The quarterback with the most touchdown passes also has the most interceptions. The baseball players with the most homeruns have also been struck out the most times. The basketball players with the most points also have the most missed shots.

In all areas of life we must embrace appropriate risk. Too often people are trapped because of a fear of failure. In dreading something bad, it becomes too easy to accept current unpleasantries, even though that bad thing is usually just a fantasy. Think about it: How often have the things you were most worried about come to pass when you decided to take a risk? Yet, how many times have you endured something you didn't have to simply because you were afraid of the unknown?

In our sport it is risky to push hard early in a race. "What if I die?" seems to be the common mantra. It is also risky to try a new event or to speed up 3/4 of the way into a race when already exhausted. But, nearly every time I've seen your children do something amazing, whether in practice or in races, it is the result of taking a risk—of deciding that failure is better than not knowing if they can succeed.

Your children should be applauded for this courage. They have much to teach us.

53

Aristotle once said, "We are what we repeatedly do. Excellence, therefore, is not an act but a habit." While true in life, this is especially true in our sport. We repeat and repeat and repeat the same motions over and over so that our muscle memory allows us to perform the stroke correctly in races. While we vary things with drills and by splitting up the strokes into parts, there are only four strokes that we do.

And to perform those four motions well not only takes a lot of repetition to be excellent, but lots of excellent repetition to be excellent. Like character, excellence is only demonstrated when challenged, not created. It is created in the days and weeks and months and years prior to any challenge.

Just before the Olympics, Jesse Owens said, "A lifetime of training for just 10 seconds." While it is true that the training we do in our sport often pinnacles with a few minutes of racing, and how that training is performed will determine the athlete's outcome in a race, I slightly disagree with this quote.

Our sport is about much more than just racing. Swimmers tend to be a different type of people than the rest of the population. One example: In high school and college, swimmers have some of the highest GPAs of all athletes. I believe it is because in order to succeed and stay with our sport long term, dedication and motivation must come from within.

I say "must" because we are in one of the hardest working and lowest glory sports. There are very few external rewards that would make someone want to become a swimmer. I mean, even while racing you spend most of the time looking at the pool bottom unable to see or hear anyone cheering.

But, since it is so internal, the attributes gained carry over into all areas of an athlete's life.

Excellent repetition of attitude at the pool will lead to excellence in life.

54

Nathaniel Emmons said, "Habit is either the best of servants or the worst of masters." For those in our sport who persist in doing things correctly, these habits tend to serve by allowing close races to be won, and personal bests to fall week after week. For those who insist on doing things "their own way" or who wish not to put forth the effort, habits tend to produce disappointment and frustration.

There are approximately three weeks left until our Regional meet—the last opportunity to qualify for the state competition. Most experts state that it takes a minimum of about three weeks to break an old habit and create a new one. We are presented with a unique opportunity to rid ourselves of self-defeating behaviors in time to perform well at the championship meet.

When I look at your children, I see quite a bit of potential. We have numerous athletes on the cusp of qualifying for the state meet. What happens over the next three weeks will greatly determine how much of this potential is actualized. However, even if nobody else qualifies for the state meet, our team and your children will be all the better for having tried. Your child will be a winner for engaging in the struggle.

And this is one of the beauties of sport. It exemplifies aspects of life, and I can think of all sorts of applications in this world, but I want to talk about the most important one. Many of us, even those who are free from the power and penalty of sin, are still enslaved by our habits. We still live in the presence of sin. Unless we willfully pray and discipline ourselves, the old habits come back. I have seen far too many people quit on God when the reality is they quit on themselves. They wanted a miracle without the work. They wanted a magic pill. They wanted to be the lord over God. In short, they wanted it "their own way."

But that isn't how it works. There can be no growth without struggle. There can be no victory without a fight. We are saved by grace alone, through faith alone, because Jesus fought for us. In thanksgiving for that gift, we should desire to abandon our worldly habits for eternal ones.

55

I heard a great quote from one of the assistant coaches at NCAA swimming powerhouse Auburn University. "The person who is willing to suffer the most will always win." Usually we associate suffering with something bad, but anyone who has ever raced in any sport can tell you that a race is about being able to push yourself to places you never thought you could go. Often times, the victory isn't to the swift, but to the one who is willing to keep on fighting. In a sort of morbid way, it is like two or more individuals trying to make each other hurt until one of them quits, or decides not to push any harder.

Much suffering must also take place before the race ever happens. Working hard in practice produces suffering, but those willing to suffer the most at practice will improve the most. They will also have the mental edge come race time.

Sometimes even choosing to go to practice is suffering, especially when you could be at home relaxing, or when you have to miss something fun to get in both homework and practice. But those who choose to come to practice will reap the most rewards. The following has been quoted so many times that nobody even knows the original author anymore. "The greater the suffering, the greater the reward."

I don't think that quote is referring to ribbons, medals, or trophies.

56

Maria Robinson said, "Nobody can go back and start a new beginning, but anyone can start today and make a new ending." This quote holds true, not just during the first week of practice, but throughout the entire season. This is a fitting theme for our season. However, one of the reasons it fits for the start of a season is that at this point we have the most control over the ending, whatever our goals may be.

As I've mentioned, while I love the sport of swimming, I do not think it is very important. However, as a tool to help raise young ladies and gentlemen of character and virtue, I find it immensely useful. This is one philosophy that separates us from other programs. We may have flaws, but this is our goal.

The most important new beginning we have is when we give our hearts and life to the Lord Jesus Christ. We are at that moment a literal new creation. The ending has changed from an eternity of misery to an eternity of joy.

But often we stagnate along the way. Sometimes we even return to our old way of doing things (like a dog to its vomit). We can do nothing apart from God, yet He uses our free will to advance His kingdom and make changes in us. I encourage you to take that part of your life that the Holy Spirit has been trying to get you to work on and start a new beginning with it today!

You can't wait. How you live your days IS how you will live your life, and if you wait for a better time to let God get ahold of you and change you, it will never happen.

Imagine yourself on your deathbed. How do you want to be remembered? Make that ending come true by acting today.

57

Jim Rohn said, "Don't join an easy crowd. You won't grow. Go where the expectations and the demands to perform are high." In life we all know this to be true. If you have ever been a part of a group that waits for good things to happen, or a group that feels they are entitled to good things without hard work, then you know what it means to stagnate. Watching and waiting and expecting others to do for you is a terrible life plan.

It is also a poor plan on any type of sports team. Up to this point in the season, we have been building a base of technique and aerobic fitness. Some athletes did not take advantage of this. I heard comments like "I'll practice more (or I'll bring my children to practice more) when we start working harder." I've also seen people whose actions seem to betray a mindset of "Stroke X is hard, so I won't focus on learning it." These types of thoughts are essentially like trying to do things the easy way and then expecting life to give you a freebie. To expect excellence, without paying attention to the mundane, is foolish.

A Special Forces instructor at Lackland Air Force base said, "Most of what we do is focus on the little boring things. That way, when the excitement starts, you don't have to worry about it." If we spend six weeks as a team learning and refining strokes, and everyone takes her responsibility seriously, then we don't have to worry about silly things at meets like "Two hand touches in butterfly" or "Make sure you keep your hands shoulder width apart." We can focus on the fun part – going fast!

The good news is that we still have time left in the season. Those who have grown in the past will continue to do so, by building on what they've learned so far. Those who haven't can still do well by taking advantage of opportunities in the present.

I am reminded that there is no such thing as a "make-up opportunity," simply a missed one. It is crucial that we don't turn one missed opportunity into two.

58

Our results are based upon what we put in. There must be realism in our expectations if we are to remain happy. Once we wrote on the board, "If you don't like what is happening, change it. You're not a tree." If your child is not satisfied with their level, there is something they can do about it! (But, if your child is happy, then we are happy as well. Not everyone wants to be a state champion swimmer.)

Regardless of your child's situation, help them to avoid comparisonitis! Nothing leads to frustration faster than a child comparing himself to another child. There are so many circumstances that make comparing one person with another unfair, that we need to avoid it – not to mention the results that can occur like jealousy, frustration, feeling superior, etc. If you think of our team as a single body, with many parts that have different functions and purposes, that may help.

One part is no less important than another. A pinkie toe may seem insignificant, but I'd like to keep mine! An appendix may seem worthless to the body, but it has been shown to have very important immunological functions when our system is compromised. In fact, there is no such thing as a "vestigial organ." Every part of us matters and every person on our team matters! (Sometimes it is sad that this isn't realized until a part is gone.)

Everyone matters on the Orca swim team. "Comparisonitis" is a disease that can make us very sick. The vaccine is focusing on yourself and how you fit into the program.

59

Seneca once said, "Luck is what happens when preparation meets opportunity." The children have been preparing themselves all season. They will get out what they put in. It will be fun to see what happens with their swimming in the championship meets. Remember, we can't control others, only ourselves. As such, we need to make sure our goals are internally, and not externally, based.

Catching the good that is within our reach is one of the finest gifts we can teach our children. Unfortunately, many opportunities in our lives are missed, because they disguise themselves as work or inconvenience. But we can only get out what we put in, and if we want a big reward we have to put in the effort!

This is true of our work life and our spiritual life, as well. I know people who claim to desire closeness with God, but they don't pray. They don't do Bible study. They don't listen to Christian music. Their reasoning is that they would do it IF they felt that closeness to God. They've reversed the order! You can't get close to someone if you don't let him into your life.

God can reveal His love to us in amazing ways causing us to seek Him. But more often than not, those "lucky" people who feel closeness to Jesus have spent time in the "dark night of the soul," and have taken advantage of opportunity.

60

R ecently, I had time to reflect on the many choices we have in our life. There is an old saying that "true freedom is not in having many choices, but in having the ability to make the right choice." I would add that part of this includes the wisdom to make the right choice. One of the unfortunate ironies of our culture is that the expansion of choices has led to a diminished sense that any of the choices matter very much. Everything starts to seem optional, and so things seem less real, because nothing seems limited or necessary.

Thomas di Zengotita wrote "Haunting the moment of 'I can experience whatever I want' is the moment of 'What difference does it make,' because this moment, the moment of the shrug is essential to our mobility among the options." Many people falsely believe that expanding options is one of the keys to happiness, that what one does is less important than the fact that one chooses to do it. So they hop from one thing to the next as soon as the honeymoon phase is over. Or they try to become a jack of all trades (master of none) thinking this will bring bliss.

In reality, those who master specific skills and take pride in a job well done are those who, in all cultures regardless of place in history, are accorded great respect and success. Detached coolness looks great in the movies, but having a purpose with convictions, and then working hard to improve, will take you much farther. And, in our culture, make you stand out.

This is the difference between instant consumption and time-consuming production. I think most of us understand this, but here are some thoughts you may not have had: Instant consumption believes in talent; time-consuming production believes in the truth of hard work and putting effort into improvement. Instant consumption is suspicious of anything that is not new; time-consuming production concerns itself with how things develop in history. Instant consumption has no long term plan or concept of cause and reaction; time-consuming production understands that many good things take time to happen, and that along the way there is a process that must be undergone so that the foundation is not shaky. Instant consumption is concerned with quick opinions (often adopting or copying those of others); time-consuming production realizes that you don't need an opinion right away, that it is better to cultivate a carefully formed idea. Instant consumption believes that wisdom is a set of rules or a ten-step process; time-consuming production knows that wisdom is more of a matter of posture towards the world and is a task that is never complete.

Unfortunately, instant consumption has also fallen to include religion. There are so many false teachers within the church that cater to our culture. People eat it up because they tell us what we want to hear, instead of the truth of the Bible. There are so many people who make themselves the ultimate authority, and think they can pick and choose from Christianity and other religions and the opinions of the world, and not be harmed. They are deluded.

We must always stand up for the truth. We must defend the faith against heresy. We must embrace church discipline and accountability. We must make a pact with one another to watch out for one another and call each other on our garbage, especially false ideas. Lastly, we must realize that ALL of our choices matter in this world.

One of the choices you made was to join our team. Maybe you knew that drowning is the leading cause of accidental death among children and wanted to guard against that tragedy. Maybe you knew that your child's aerobic foundation for the rest of his or her life is set through the pubescent years. Maybe you knew that the average lifespan of an NFL football player is 54 years old, and you wanted your child to have something they can enjoy well into their later years. Maybe you wanted your child to be with friends, or to share your love of swimming, or to learn values, or a host of other reasons. Whatever your reason, we hope you feel like you made the right choice, and we appreciate your communication as we seek to improve our program.

61

There is an old African proverb that states, "God makes three requests of his children: Do the best you can, where you are, with what you have, now."

For those of you who don't know my philosophy on meets, the above proverb is a very good summary of my expectations. Orcas does not expect perfect performances. We expect some failures and disappointments. We expect anxiety. We expect some uncomfortableness while being challenged. But regardless, we expect your children to do the best they can with what they know at that particular moment.

This is one of the neat ways in which swimming, and athletics in general, can help prepare your children to have a strong and positive mindset in all areas of their life. Races, and even difficult practices, give us a place to draw strength from when we're being challenged, because we've been challenged before. It isn't always fun to feel like the underdog, but in athletics every person will experience it at some point in time. So later in life when your children are at a job interview, or taking a difficult exam, or going through a tough time with their family, they know that will come out of it okay – often better than what they first thought. And even if they don't, they will know how to handle disappointment with maturity, and not shrink when another opportunity presents itself.

In short, your children will do honor to the Creator and to themselves through such perseverance.

62

Peter Beale said, "Heroes know that things must happen when it is time for them to happen. A quest may not simply be abandoned…a happy ending cannot come in the middle of the story."

Sometimes, we forget that there are truly such things as heroes. Even more often we forget that most of us are a hero to somebody (like our children!). Even the most mundane of chores is a quest. How something is done is more important than we usually believe. There may be no parades or knighting ceremonies when we shovel the driveway, pay the bills, or take out time to play with our kids, but those actions have an effect on the little people who want to someday grow up to be "just like you."

I encourage you to never abandon your quest, and to find a truly happy ending. You will notice that there aren't many stories where the happy ending is a large retirement – it is finding love, peace, fulfillment through service to a higher cause, and contentment in the areas of life we once took for granted. The ultimate happy ending comes when Jesus tells us "Well done."

On swim team we talk about finishing strong in order to have a happy ending. I hope that everyone comes to as many practices as possible before this season ends, so that even if you can't race at our last meet, you will be able to finish strong.

63

Over Christmas, I visited my in-laws in Florida. While there someone told me, "I wish everyone were more like farmers." Having grown up on a farm here in Wisconsin, I asked what was meant by the comment. "Well," he answered, "too many people try to reap what they don't sow. If you don't plant any seeds, you can't expect a crop. And you can't expect a different crop from the one you planted."

This is true in life, as well as it is true in swimming. Without naming names, every season when there are about two weeks left, I tend to get a group of kids who suddenly want to go to state or they share with me a goal time for the last meet of the season. I usually tell them that we'll do our best, but the beginning of the season is the time to make such plans, not the end. And, though I've seen improvement in those children, I have yet to see one reach their goal.

Other times I have children tell me about their goals at the beginning of the season, but then they do little in the way of follow-up. They too tend to be disappointed with the result. These children were just wishing; they weren't really goal setting.

Finally, I have had parents want to know why their child, who only averages one practice per week, isn't swimming on a relay at championship meets. These are like believers, who show up frequently on Sunday morning, and the rest of the time lead lives no different from the rest of the world. Yet they can't figure out why they don't feel close to God or why their faith doesn't seem to be "working." They lack dedication.

In all the above circumstances, there was an expectation to cash in on a crop that wasn't planted.

64

I would like to continue to focus on the theme (and Orca value) of dedication. In every season, not just in sports, but in every season of our life, there are a limited number of opportunities. And once they are gone, they are gone forever.

In swimming we say, "There is no such thing as a 'make-up' practice. What's missed is missed." Those who are successful tend to be those individuals who are dedicated to making the most of the opportunities they have. It is so easy to get lost in the mindset of "missing this doesn't matter," because it seems like there is always another practice, another season, another year. But there is not. All things end.

Michael Landon said, "Someone should tell us in the beginning that we are dying. That way we live each day to the fullest. Do it I say! There are only so many tomorrows."

There are two mistakes we humans tend to make if we ever even get to the point of trying to live life to the fullest. The first is that we live for the wrong thing; we tend to focus on that which is meaningless. The second is that we are unfocused and try to do a little bit of everything, only to find out later that our world rewards specialists, not generalists (Jack of all trades, master of none as the old adage goes).

This is not to say that your child should only do swimming, or that we shouldn't explore our options. However, it is very important to learn early that when an option is selected, we must be dedicated to it so that we get the most out it. In that way, our choices have real meaning and require real responsibility.

65

Most of you have probably heard the quote, "Faith can move mountains." Some people confuse faith and belief with wishful thinking. It is true, you can't just wish away a mountain. You can't wish yourself into the state swim meet. You can't wish yourself into a new car or a higher paying job. But belief produces a positive attitude which generates the power, skill, and energy to act.

Acting on faith pushes an individual beyond the boundaries of average.

We know the statistics. Most people in leadership positions or high paying jobs are not extraordinary. They are ordinary people who believed in their own self-worth enough to act. I have heard many swimmers say, "Coach, I want to go to state." I tell them that this is fantastic, and usually give them some advice on how to get there. But, if patterns of behavior don't change – many missed practices, goofing off, absence of maximum effort, etc. – I know that they are in the category of wishful thinkers, instead of believers.

I have seen a lot of regrets from wishful thinkers, but very few from believers, even if they don't reach their ultimate goal. To wishful thinkers the end result is the reward. They want something because of what they think that something will do to them. For example, they want to win state because they think that will bring them happiness. But people who believe in themselves and act upon their goals realize that the ultimate reward was the journey. Though it produces elation, sometimes attaining the goal is the least significant part of the process.

Now, if this is true of this life, what about the life to come? I have seen many wishful thinkers who want to do great things for the Lord. First, this assumes that God is this little being that somehow needs us, and that is utterly false. But second, they never seem to get around to it, because they have little faith and instead of being a mature Christian, they stay infants. I have heard it said, "They have been a Christian for 20 years – and in all 20 of them they lived in year one." These people need to change their behaviors and the patterns of their life to become more like Jesus.

The one difference between sports and the gospel is that all true believers will get eternity in the end, and the reward is better than the journey. Yet, even that said, the reward is greater for those who journeyed well!

66

Someone once said, "It is better to build strong children than to try to repair damaged adults." This strongly correlates to the biblical proverb, "Train up a child in the way he should go; even when he is old he will not depart from it." If we train up our children well, they will be strong adults. If we train them up poorly, they will be damaged adults.

This is one of the reasons the Orcas have chosen a values-based approach to coaching children. Swimming is merely a means to this end. Instead of hoping that kids will pick up ideals, such as discipline and perseverance, we want to start there and hope they will add them to their swimming. For those who don't know, our values are Spirit, Sportsmanship, Dedication, Motivation, and Excellence.

I have come to realize how important parents are to this process. Unfortunately, many in our culture minimize the importance of the parental role without realizing it. For example, I have heard parents say they didn't bring their child to practice because the child "didn't feel like it" or "didn't want to go." Then the parent proceeds to ask me to motivate their child so that their child will want to come to practice.

Really? Where is the good training in that request? Where is the role of parent? What are we teaching our children with this model?

First, children aged 5, 8, 12, or 16 years old don't know anything about life or what's best for them. So, why is their opinion paramount? Should we allow them to waste our time and money?

Second, when the most important person in the world to a child (mom or dad) says or acts like something doesn't matter, how can they expect a coach to make it matter? When it is something the parent wants deep down, why aren't they teaching it? A coach can't teach lessons or values, we can only reinforce what is expected at home. A coach can only be effective if mom or dad is FIRST acting like the mom or dad.

Finally, what if parents strongly believe in the values, but are inconsistent in holding their children accountable to them? Inconsistency teaches kids that values are only there when it is convenient. It teaches that the value really isn't valued. If you preach dedication, yet aren't dedicated, or allow your child to get away with being undedicated, then you have failed because your child has been taught, through your actions, that this value isn't important. Likewise, if you profess to believe something, and then pick and choose what values to follow, then children will realize this inconsistency and question why ANY of it matters if it is so easy to be flippant about one point.

So, how do we accomplish this?

To begin, we need to improve practice attendance. If your child doesn't come to practice, they won't improve. It is funny how many people every season get so close to making it to state and say, "I would have made it if I would have gone to more practices" or "if I would have worked harder." I don't know about everyone else, but I'm tired of hearing about "ifs."

We also have to increase loyalty to the club. It is hard to be excited about anything, if you are not loyal to it. This is an area where parents play a huge role. If you're not excited about your child's swimming, they won't be excited. If you don't bring your child to practice, they can't improve. If your children don't swim in meets, they lose sight of why they have to go to practice. If you don't reinforce goals, standards, and values, they will not be adhered to by your children. Get excited.

Youth sports are fun, and they are even more fun as your children improve, and as the team improves!

At the start of the season, we challenged the children to do something that will help them get just a little bit better every single day. Remember, you do not become great all of a sudden. It creeps up on you almost without your noticing it by 1/10 of second here or 1/10 of a second there – whether in swimming or in other areas of your life.

But all too often, people don't do anything to get better. It is action, not intellectual agreement, that makes all the difference.

67

Since this is my last parent's letter of the season, I want to say on behalf of all the coaches and board members, "Thank you for a great Orca season!" I am so grateful for the opportunity to work with your children and be a small part of your family. It is fun to see improvement, win medals and trophies, and participate in championship meets.

But my greatest joy as a coach is simply being a part of your children's lives. I know I can speak for all of the coaches when I say that we tend to get just as much out of a season as the children do. They are wonderful, and we must remember that we only have them for a little while.

Socrates wrote, "Could I climb the highest place in Athens, I would lift up my voice and proclaim, 'Fellow citizens, why do you burn and scrape every stone to gather wealth, and take so little care of your children to whom you must one day relinquish all?'"

Thank you for caring for your children. Please, never underestimate the value of YOUR time with them. As my grandfather often said, "Spend time with your children while they are young, so that they will spend time with you when you are old."

68

"Good swimmers train hard. Great swimmers train thoughtful." I borrowed this motto from an interview I read with Bob Bowman (Michael Phelps' coach). In the interview, Bowman stated that in the United States alone there were probably tens of thousands of people with just as much genetic capability as Phelps. He also stated that there were probably thousands of people who swim just as much, and work just as hard, as Phelps does. Likely, the overlap between genetics and hard work still leaves us with several hundred people in the United States who are physically just as prepared as Phelps is.

The biggest difference between Michael Phelps and other people is the thoughtfulness he puts into each stroke.

Shortly after I read that interview, I saw another with Katie Hoff. In the interview she said the only reason she made it to her current level is because she never pushed off a wall without a goal for improving, and she never takes a single stroke without a plan.

This season, more than any other in the past, we coaches will be focused on what your children are focused on. We are going to, age appropriately, encourage more concentration and expenditure of mental energy.

Some people when they first hear this think that it will lead to less enjoyment for the children. As such, I want to quote at length from Mihaly Csikszentmihalyi, former professor and chairman of the Dept. of Psychology at the University of Chicago and expert on optimal experiences and enjoyment.

As our studies have suggested, the phenomenology of enjoyment has eight major components. When people reflect on how it feels when their experience is most positive, they mention at least one, and often all of the following. First, the experience usually occurs when we confront tasks we have a chance of completing. Second, we must be able to concentrate on what we are doing. Third and fourth, the concentration is usually possible because the task undertaken has clear goals and provides immediate feedback. Fifth, one acts with a deep but effortless involvement that removes from awareness the worries and frustrations of everyday life. Sixth, enjoyable experiences allow people to exercise a sense of control over their actions. Seventh, concern for the self disappears, yet paradoxically the sense of self emerges stronger after the [enjoyable] experience is over. Finally, the sense of the duration of time is altered; hours pass by in minutes, and minutes can stretch out to seem like hours. The combination of all these elements causes a sense of deep enjoyment that is so rewarding people feel that expending a great deal of energy is worthwhile simply to be able to feel it.

Swimming thoughtfully is thus a perfect conduit for excellence AND enjoyment!

69

For all of human history, there have been little quips and sayings that have helped people gain wisdom and learn how to live well. These are called proverbs. They have always been a part of helping children improve their intellect and grow to become wise adults. Most people don't realize this, but the book of Proverbs in the Bible was actually written for educating children. By the way, a great way to gain wisdom by the way is to read one chapter of Proverbs a day as a family for one month.

What is common about most proverbs like "a stitch in time saves nine," (this is not from the Bible) is that they don't come right out and tell you what they mean. Rather you think about what they mean, and then apply them to a variety of situations. If we just said, "Sew your shirt now before the hole gets bigger," it doesn't have the same effect and won't apply to other situations. Also, because you have to think about them, and, because they are often clever or have some type of imagery, they are memorable and not easily forgotten.

Some people have asked me why swimmers tend to do so many drills. Drills are similar to proverbs. They help the body gain "swimming wisdom" and often apply to a variety of situations. As coaches, we tell the swimmers things directly like "head down" or "rotate" or "focus on X," but, when we give the swimmers drills to do, the stroke flaws often get fixed almost magically. Backstroke drills can fix freestyle problems, and many butterfly drills help in all the other strokes. Instead of changing a bad habit by attacking it directly, we take an indirect approach which fixes the problem without resistance.

The other interesting thing about drills is that no matter how many years a person swims, they always can improve with drills, and many people are helped by the drills they learned back when they were children. I know that if something isn't quite right with my stroke, it is time to do some drills to correct it before it gets worse. And I've also seen other lap swimmers doing drills to prevent stroke flaws.

We must always remember that we are never stagnant for long – we are either getting better or getting worse. This is true of all areas of our life and it is true of our growth in the faith. We must be diligent in pursuing Christ-likeness at all times. After all, "a stitch in time saves nine."

70

Robert Ingersoll once said, "In nature there are neither rewards nor punishments – there are consequences." This seems to be true in sports, as well. Rewards and punishments may be a side effect of the consequences, but the important things happen long before any competitions. There are positive consequences to good practice attendance, taking care of yourself, and practicing with a purpose. There are negative consequences to things like laziness, going through the motions, and poor diet.

Unfortunately, there seems to be a victim mentality running rampant in our society. In sports, as in life, there is great power in taking responsibility for all that happens to us. Sure, a lot of things happen to us out of our control, but how we deal with those things will determine our success or failure. Motivation, one of our Orca values, can be defined as taking responsibility for all aspects of your life.

A motivated person will defeat a "talented" person every time. In fact, I prefer to define talent based on motivation because, especially in age group sports, development plays such a large role. So while "talented" may see early success, motivated individuals see success later on when it counts the most. A six-foot tall 11-year old may win a lot now, but how they do later, when everyone else is six-feet tall, depends upon their motivation.

I want to encourage all of our athletes, and you parents (as their number one supporters) to be motivated in taking responsibility for your swimming. Coaches do a great deal, but we aren't the ones in the water.

There are consequences to your actions. In balancing our lives we have to determine what consequences we are willing to live with. Then we need to look at our current life and decide, "should I be content or do I need to make a change?"

71

I read a quote that said, "The most important thing about having a goal is having one." I would add that this goal should be edifying and God glorifying.

Regardless of your reasons for having your child swim, take the time to talk to your children about their reasons for swimming and what they hope to accomplish. This will help your child to focus on what they want to do in our sport. "To have fun" or "to swim fast" is pretty generic. Get them to specify – "What do you mean by fast?" Then, ask your child what they think they should be doing to get what they want.

Spend some time asking how their goal gives honor to their Creator. Make sure they see how it helps them grow as a person.

As parents you are your child's number one fan, and the person with whom they most want to share things. This will help you take an active interest in what they are doing, while at the same time keeping the responsibility on the child (telling them their goals or how they should get them tends to be far less effective than the child figuring it out – even if you have to drop some helpful hints). Later, follow up with them to see how things are going and to see if they are doing what they know they should be.

This keeps everyone motivated.

72

The other day I heard someone say, "Today is the youngest you will ever be. Take advantage of it." I remember in the past thinking things like, "If it takes five years to get good at playing piano, I'll be almost 30 years old before I'm proficient. It's not worth it." Now I think about how if I would have dedicated myself to that task, I would be proficient now for five years instead of being exactly where I was then.

Five years from now, we will wish we had pursued those goals that we could have accomplished had we started today. Ten years from now, we will all look back at how much energy we have at this moment and wish we still had that much "get up and go." Fifteen years from now, we will marvel at how much time we wasted, when we could have been doing important things. Twenty years from now, we will either be bitter or joyous about the memories we made and the things we accomplished.

I often think about how easy it is as a child to work towards being excellent at something. Sure there is school, and hopefully some responsibilities at home, but really most of what holds a child back is either a lack of focus, lack of desire, or quite simply sheer laziness. I am a firm believer in a kid taking the time to be a kid. Children need to play and goof around and imagine and socialize. But we all know that their potential right now towards becoming excellent at something is far greater than it will be when they take on adult responsibilities.

So, first, I want you to encourage them. They don't realize their potential. Sometimes we may even have to be the "mean" parent and help them stay dedicated. Second, I want to encourage you, because you too are the youngest you will ever be. Show your children by example what it means to seize the day. Finally, I offer a bit of warning, don't seize the day at the expense of having quality time with your child. Otherwise your accomplishment will become regret. There must be a balance to our improvement.

73

There is a famous Hopi saying that states, "You can't even pick up a pebble with one finger." The point of this proverb has nothing to do with gathering pebbles, but has everything to do with teamwork.

The American culture seems to value the lone individual who picked himself up by his own bootstraps, and then defied all the odds to become a sensation.

Of course, this is a Hollywood myth. Nobody who became successful at any level has ever done so alone. Granted the individual has done many things that "ordinary people" were unwilling to do. But ultimately, if that person did those extraordinary things while in isolation, their efforts would go unrecognized.

This is true in our sport, just as it is in life. Swimming seems like it is an individual sport, because on race day the athlete stands alone on the blocks. However, the swimmer is not alone. There is a team that has surrounded that individual and profoundly influenced that person. In many ways, the team determines the outcome of that individual's race.

How does a team do this? I will highlight three ways.

The first way is attitude. We all know that "a little yeast leavens the whole batch." If there is a supportive, encouraging, and positive attitude on a team, the individual is more likely to do their best and maximize their potential, especially when faced with difficult challenges.

The second way is companionship. Not only is it more enjoyable to have friends with you while working out, but they also make you push yourself to places you couldn't or wouldn't be willing to go by yourself.

The third way is accountability. No one likes being told to clean up their act. Nobody finds it pleasant to be asked to stop messing around and do the right thing. Very few people like to have their faults brought to light. But these are all necessary if growth is going to take place. If coaches help with this, it is one thing, but when there is constructive accountability among peers, the results are astounding.

The most successful individuals are surrounded by teams (this is one reason we MUST be a part of a local church). We have often talked about how to be a successful individual, so today I want to ask all of our athletes, "Are you being a good teammate by helping to elevate others?"

74

Janine Caffrey, EdD, said that the sure sign of an overscheduled child is a child who is constantly bored if you don't provide him or her with something to do. Other researchers have noted that one of the biggest reasons children are not motivated is because they do not have enough time to do nothing.

I want to talk briefly about the importance of encouraging creativity and imagination in producing motivation. Without creativity and imagination children don't want to do things or become things. Think about it. If your child isn't given a chance to imagine his future or to play different roles or to creatively think about life, how can he ever decide what he wants to do with his life?!

The best way to promote creativity and imagination is to make sure at least a couple of hours every day are unstructured. Leave the children to their own devices, so that they can play and simply be kids. This behavior is inherent and innate. Children are designed to be free-roaming and to engage in spontaneous play.

Without free time used to develop imagination, all children will learn is that they are to robotically traverse the system each and every day. The system has merely promised them that if they do X, Y, and Z they will be able to get a job and enter a new system. That is not living!

Once I asked a swimmer what he wanted to do with his life. He responded that he didn't know. I asked him, "Why are you going to college then?"

He replied, "Because that's next."

How sad to have no direction, dreams, wishes, or goals!

A motivated individual will use the system to find happiness and pursue excellence. But without unstructured time to explore, be creative, and use her imagination, she is hard pressed to decide WHAT will make her happy. She will also find it difficult to know whether or not she has achieved excellence without someone else telling her.

Additionally, if every single aspect of a child's life is structured and scheduled, he will never have the need to use the part of his brain that figures out what is interesting and exciting, and how to pursue it. He will not have time to reflect on his day in order to evaluate and improve. In short, he won't grow.

Unstructured time is vital for your child to develop dreams and to determine the actions necessary to pursue his or her purpose and find meaning in life.

75

Calvin Coolidge once remarked, "No person was ever honored for what he received. Honor has been the reward for what he gave."

It has been interesting over the years to watch the dynamics of our swim team. While it is true that often times the better swimmers earn everyone's respect, there are also plenty of instances where they do not. I have also noticed that there are many athletes of average ability whom even the best swimmers look up to.

The common thread uniting the most respected Orcas has always been giving. Honored teammates are always those who work hard in practice, giving of themselves. Esteemed swimmers are those who give to others by encouraging, building up, and being otherwise helpful to those around them. These athletes are also the ones who give to the team at a larger level by volunteering, referring others to the program, and living out the Orca Way.

On the flip side, the least respected athletes – even those who swim fast – are the ones who are self-seeking. They want the accolades. They will sacrifice others to help themselves. They backstab. They even work hard trying to appear as if they are a giving person, so that others will notice and praise them. Sometimes they even pride themselves in how poorly they behave, listen, or practice. Glory seekers will ruin a team.

Obviously, this is true in our lives outside of the swimming pool, as well. This is one reason giving in a church setting is supposed to remain anonymous. Giving is supposed to be for others, not ourselves! But in the end, God reveals our heart and along the way, the most respected people are often those not seeking respect.

76

I am reminded of an old saying that states, "True nobility is being superior to your previous self." In swimming, this means that we can't be satisfied with a certain level of technique mastery or with our past performances.

With that in mind, the question for Orcas is, "Where do we go from here?"

Certainly there is nothing noble about resting on our laurels. We have room to grow, and this can be done by fixing the things that didn't work out for us, and continuing to improve those areas that brought us success. Luckily for us, we still have time to improve!

Keep in mind that anything noble is never easy. If it were easy, everyone would be doing it. To deliberately look for something to fix, and make it better, takes effort. It is the road less traveled because it is mentally taxing and physically demanding.

In order to capitalize on the remaining weeks of the season, our athletes need to show up – both physically and mentally. The coaches envision that your children will demonstrate nobility during the second half of the season, so that we can finish better than our previous selves.

77

Recently, some people on our team asked me why I talk about God so much. The strange part is that the people who asked claim to be followers of Jesus. This reminded me that, all too often in our culture, believers have forgotten Jesus' words in Matthew 12:30: "Whoever is not with me is against me, and whoever does not gather with me scatters."

It is not necessary for something to be in opposition to Christ to be against him. Let me repeat that. It is not necessary for something to be in opposition to Christ to be against him. You don't have to actively interfere with the work of Jesus to scatter.

I don't want to be legalistic but there are far too many Christians in America, and dare I say our city, who think we can be neutral, who believe there are things in this world that are just neutral - that we don't need to bring up God all of the time.

Neutral really means "this particular thing without God is just fine." We teach this to our children. Watching the Super Bowl without God is fine. Learning history without God is fine. Celebrating the beauty of a sunset without God is fine. Buying a bottle of ketchup without God is fine. Becoming a good athlete or learning to play a musical instrument without God is fine. Going to work or handling business without God is fine. Celebrating Christmas or other holidays without God is fine. Going to the doctor without God is fine. Giving money to help the poor without God is fine.

Even when we don't say it verbally, how often do our actions tell our children or non-believers that most of the time God is not part of our lives?

How often do we put our kids in an environment where we are essentially telling them that this attitude is okay? How often do we excuse ourselves with the thought that "this doesn't matter?"

It all matters when you are living in a world ruled by the devil.

Neutrality is against God. Therefore, in fact really, there is no true neutrality; Jesus is trying to make that clear. What we perceive as neutral is to be friends with the world . . . if you believe what Jesus says.

Don't confuse freedom in Christ with the concept of being neutral. We can focus on being good swimmers because we have freedom in Christ. *How* we become good swimmers, and what we say along the way, indicates if we are gathering with Christ or if we believe "this particular aspect of the world is just fine without God."

78

Martin Luther King Jr. once said, "If you are called to be a street sweeper, sweep streets even as Michelangelo painted, or Beethoven composed music, or Shakespeare wrote poetry. Sweep streets so well that all the hosts of heaven and earth will pause to say, 'Here lived a great street sweeper who did his job well.'"

In life, we don't get a lot of choices regarding to the hand that is dealt us. We can't choose our parents, where we are born, what our culture is, what our talents are, and what our weaknesses are. In fact, we get surprisingly few important choices when you sit back and think about it. However, what I love about Dr. King's quotation is that even though we often don't get a choice in the matter, the one thing that we can always control is how we respond to that which happens to us. And that, perhaps, is the most powerful and important choice of all.

No matter what our situation is, we can always control our attitude. It is the one thing that people EXPECT us to be responsible for and what society holds us accountable. Someone may have a tragic life and prosper as is the case with David Pelzer. He suffered horrible child abuse and became a successful person. While others have everything handed to them on a silver platter and they ruin themselves as is the case with far too many celebrities.

Attitude tends to turn the tide of "luck" for better or for worse. My prayer for all of you is that you take responsibility for your lives and all that happens to you – even more so in those areas of your life where you have a choice. But, as my car insurance company once said, "You are partially liable, simply because you were there."

My prayer for all of our swimmers is that they take responsibility for the sport and their results. No matter how good or bad a coach is, or how many toys they have to use, or what type of pool they are in your son or daughter is ultimately the one in the water swimming and is the only one who has a decent amount of control over their fate and what they take away from the sport.

WORLDVIEW PART TWO

79

It is hard to believe that five weeks of the season are already complete. I could see improvement as early as the first week, because our swimmers became more thoughtful about what they are doing. In trying to help our swimmers become more thoughtful, I have often asked the question, "Which stroke is the most important?" I have gotten many answers, but over time most have realized there is only one correct answer, "the one you are currently taking."

"The one you are currently taking" is the only one in each swimmer's control. It is the only one that affects the future, as it indicates if they are going to improve or get worse. It is the only one they can change if needed. It is the one that determines what happens. Ultimately, it is the only one that matters.

I hope our swimmers realize that this mentality is true in life, as well. Which test question is the most important? "The one you are currently answering." Which part of your job is the most important? "The part you are currently doing." Which person is the most important? "The person you are currently with." What is the most important thing in the world? "The thing you are currently working on or participating in."

When we swim, we shouldn't be thinking about school. When we are at school, we shouldn't be thinking about swimming. When we are with our family, we shouldn't be thinking about our work. When we are at work, we shouldn't be thinking about our family.

The truth is, we all spend a lot of time and energy thinking about things that are either imagined or already complete or that which we can't do anything about. If we would focus on what we are currently doing, we would get it done better, faster, and with more enjoyment.

The quality of all of life's experiences are greatly enhanced when we pay attention to what we are doing in that moment.

80

This week I reflected on the idea that, in our culture, it is "normal" to be busily moving our children from one activity to the next. I also thought about how in each activity the coaches or teachers probably talk about sacrificing, so that your child can get better at their particular niche.

It dawned on me that we have confused the meaning of the word "privilege" with the word "sacrifice." Sacrifice is when a mother doesn't eat so that her children can. Sacrifice is when someone takes a bullet for someone else. Sacrifice is when a father works two jobs so that his family can have electricity. Most of us don't have a clue what it really means to sacrifice.

So, in our over-privileged society, we distort the word. Is it really a sacrifice to swim two times per day, pushing your body to its limit, so that you can post a fast time at a meet? In one small sense it is, because we forego other privileges in order to do that. Is it a sacrifice in the truest sense of the word? Not even close.

If our biggest worry is how fast we can make ourselves go from point A to point B, then we are living in the type of luxury that most of the world can't even fathom. If we call it "sacrifice" to skip the luxury of going to a movie so that we can better reap the rewards of the privilege of coming to practice, then we have lost sight of reality.

As a team, I do not want us to miss what is really important. State is coming up and yet, I find myself praying that people will sign up for the charity event, so that we can benefit Neighborhood Connection. As a team, we can do far more good than an individual, so we should take advantage of this truth.

With privilege comes great responsibility.

81

Sometimes I wish that I could go back in time and be an athlete again now that I've been a coach. I know I certainly would have listened better and put more effort into certain areas. I have come to realize that one of my biggest mistakes as an athlete was lack of submission to my coaches. As parents, I'm sure we also believe this of our children.

Like most kids, I started out submitting very well, but then as I improved, I forgot what made me successful. I began to get an elevated opinion of myself and thought I knew better than those with experience. I thought I was smarter than those who taught me the little I knew. And because of that, I didn't improve as much.

And because I didn't improve as much, my heart became more rebellious. Oddly enough, I was captain of my college swim team for two years, even though most of that time I was injured, trying to do things my own way, and while carrying that rebellion.

After college, I began to train solely for health reasons, instead of for racing. During that time, the attitude of submission came back to me. I ended up swimming some of the best times in my life, including being the second fastest Masters 100 breaststroke time in the nation. I was no longer deceived into thinking I knew what was best for me.

I should note that submission is different from obedience. Obedience is the act of following, but submission is the attitude of the heart - you can obey without submitting. Had you known my high school and college coaches, you would know why I was obedient to their faces, even when I wasn't submitting.

Thinking about it now, some of the greatest successes in my life have been the result of submitting to those in authority. Submission is why I was producing television shows when I was 23 years old. Submission is why I won a national award with the military. Submission is how I got this dream job of working with your children. On the flip side, some of the most stressful periods of my life were when I tried to justify my rebellion – and a lot of times, even to most outside observers, that rebellion probably seemed just. I had forgotten that we are all human and we all make mistakes, and they need to be handled in the proper way.

I'm not saying we should check our brains at the door and submit to whatever anyone may pronounce. Sometimes "authorities" are wrong, and need to be corrected in a dignified way. Additionally, people in authority usually don't need or want drones or "yes men." That is not true submission, though many mistakenly think this is the case.

In our culture, independence is valued highly, but often at the expense of success and well-being which can come from putting our pride aside. Submission is about respect and working together with delegated authorities to achieve the greatest possible result, and not trying to get away with something every step of the way.

I hope our older athletes learn the value of submission. To understand the importance of submission is what I hope to teach our younger athletes. This will lead to the greatest success for Orcas, and it begins with the attitude of your child's heart.

82

Unbeknownst to your children, for the past nine weeks I have been keeping track of excuses I hear as to why they have failed (often times, why they are about to fail!). In doing so, I have also noticed that the more successful an athlete is, the less inclined they are to make excuses – even during those times when the excuse borders on being a legitimate reason.

I have also noticed that these excuses tend to fall into categories, so I will share them with you as such, let you figure out how your particular one fits the bill, and offer some solutions to these failure mindsets.

It seems to me, from my floundering through life, that people who fail do so because they've given themselves a reason to fail. Those who don't fail have all of the same excuses but they recognize them either as a lie or as something they just need to deal with, all the while focusing on what they can do, instead of what they can't.

As I imagine this information is useful outside of the pool, please share it with your children. I always encourage you to share my weekly letters with your children, but this one I feel strongly enough to remind you.

Excuse #1) I'm not talented.

Most kids seem to have two errors in thinking: They overestimate other people's talent. They underestimate their own.

We all have different gifts. What matters is not how much you have, but what you do with what God gave you. I have seen a lot of very smart people use their brains to prove why things won't work or can't be done, and a lot of average people use their abilities to figure out how to succeed.

Knowledge is not power; it is only potential power. I have seen quite a few kids, with everything going for them, point to a more successful athlete on our team and whine about how they don't have the one thing that the other less gifted athlete does have. Talent (being defined as "natural ability") is not success; it is only potential success.

How do we overcome excuse #1? Don't sell yourself short. Concentrate on how to best manage what you have, and don't focus on what you don't have. Remind yourself that attitude determines altitude. Use your brain to find ways to win, and not to prove why you will lose. Value and love yourself enough to realize that you are worth success.

Excuse #2) I'm the wrong age. Or someday I'll get serious about that.

I heard a comedian once state, "I'm too young to succeed. Well, what I mean is, I'm too old to succeed. Well, I guess the problem is that I'm in that awkward age in between."

I have seen eight-year olds try to get state cuts. I have known swimmers (actually I was one of these) who couldn't swim a lick before they were 12, and then they swam at the college level or beyond. I knew a guy who went to college when he was 50 years old because he figured he'd graduate by the time he was 55, and that would give him 15 years to work in his dream job. I was producing television shows when I was 23 years old, because it never occurred to me that everyone else around me was in their 30s and 40s.

It is easy to look back at what we coulda, shoulda, and mighta done, and resign ourselves to failure because we didn't do it. It is easy to create an imaginary self that lives in the future, who easily does what we don't have the commitment to do now. Get over it! There is only now.

Some ways to overcome excuse #2: Look at your present age in a positive way. Be excited about being the youngest or oldest still able to do X. Learn from the past, but prepare for the future in the present. Look at how much productive time you have left in any given endeavor – most of us are surprised at how much opportunity there is in life. Stop thinking, "I should have started years ago" or "I will start when" and begin to think, "I'm starting right now."

Excuse #3) I have bad luck.

Nothing happens without a cause. If you believe you always swim bad at a certain pool, or that every time you're about to succeed something bad happens, then the cause is you. There is no such thing as luck. If luck were the cause of anything, then everything would fall apart. Imagine if I put our relays together based on luck of the draw, or who swims at the state meet based on throwing darts at a board.

I used to believe I had bad luck. I was in several car accidents (luckily none that were serious), was hit twice by a car while running (fortunately, in both instances I wasn't seriously hurt), and had many other fluke things that happened to me – often at a time when some type of success was on the horizon. One day, a trusted friend just said to me, "You've got to take responsibility for everything that happens to you." I replied that I just had bad luck and that a lot of those things, he had to admit, were way out of my control. He then stated, "If you were there, you had some control." He then encouraged me to simply say, "I used to have bad luck." Just that change in thought was enough to make my bad luck disappear.

Some cures for excuse #3: Accept the law of cause and effect. There is a reason for everything. As the old saying goes, "The harder I work, the luckier I get." Get rid of wishful thinking (or worse yet, rule-bending or scheming). There are no effortless ways to succeed. Success comes from doing things, and mastering principles, and learning from failure. Luck isn't a magical force out there that helps one person and hurts another. Instead of waiting for luck, work hard to develop qualities in yourself, so that others will call you lucky.

Excuse #4) Bad health.

We all get bumps and bruises and colds and things. So do Olympians. Some of us need more sleep than others. Some of us break bones. Some of us have diabetes. Some of us have asthma. Some have allergies. Some have name-your-ailment-here. There are Olympians with the exact same problems, and, more often than not, their case is worse than yours.

There is no perfect human specimen. We all have things wrong with us because we live in a fallen world. Worrying about it causes the most problems. Most successful people could use instances of bad health as an excuse for failure, but they don't.

I have heard it said that three-fourths of hospital beds are filled with people who created their own illness. This phenomena is called Emotionally Induced Illness. They are real physical manifestations that most likely originate psychosomatically. These more extreme cases begin with an innocent enough mindset of "I get sick easily" or "I don't want to overdo it" or "I'm clumsy" or "I get hurt easily" or "I'm probably going to get cancer because my father did."

This is an example that I have experienced. I used to be sick all of the time. I thought I was one of those people who naturally has a weak immune system, and that was confirmed by doctors. After I got past my belief that I had bad luck, I decided to start telling myself "I used to get sick all of the time." Viola! I started to get sick less frequently and recover more quickly from illnesses. As a result, my confidence rose and my instances of being sick went down even further. When doctors tested my immune system again I was told that it was exceptional. Nothing had changed except I decided I wasn't going to put up with my excuse anymore.

How to beat excuse #4: Refuse to talk about your health except as needed to impart information. Don't go through life comparing sufferings. Besides being a bore, it becomes almost like a woe-is-me competition which leads to worse or more severe conditions. Admit it, we all like to win competitions even if that competition is "Who has it the worst." Let people be surprised that you have X after you succeed.

Don't worry about your health. You need to be healthy and take preventative measures. But don't convince yourself you have something or are about to get something, until it is proven you've actually got it. Be grateful for how good your health is. There is always someone who has it worse. Remind yourself that life is yours to enjoy; don't pass up living by thinking yourself into a doctor's office.

83

I want to talk briefly about the number one reason children join swim teams – to have fun. There is a huge difference between having fun at the expense of excellence and having fun while pursuing excellence. As excellence is one of our core values I think this is an important point. Having fun at the expense of excellence (goofing around, not putting forth effort, ONLY coming for the games, etc) leads to poor habits and slow swimming, which ultimately equals no fun and a lot of disappointment (or even crying). Sometimes we have to put off instant gratification for a greater good!

Having fun while pursing excellence means that an athlete accepts and expects high practice standards (no whining!) and tough workouts. They find pride in doing things well and to the best of their ability. When your child walks out of the pool, they should feel like they accomplished something, not like they managed to survive or get away with something. This gives the swimmers a feeling of confidence, so they can relax in times of pressure (knowing they prepared well), and reap the rewards of personal bests and fast swims.

The difference ultimately comes down to attitude. Two individuals can do the exact same practice and one finds it fun (even if it is hard) and the other does not. The first takes responsibility for their improvement, while the second does not. The first tries to support their team in getting better; the second does not. The first looks at the big picture; the second does not. I think you get the idea.

That said, "For everything there is a season." Besides tough workouts and charity events, we do try to include deliberate fun times. My daughter (in white group) was surprised to see how many times I have fun written into the practices, IF we get our work done and IF everyone behaves properly. I believe that fun is important, but not at the expense of excellence.

84

Congratulations on another great week of swimming. You should be proud of your children's efforts. Much of their efforts the past couple of weeks have been to create new habits. A habit is simply a behavior that you keep repeating until it becomes automatic. Negative habits produce negative consequences and positive habits produce positive consequences.

This is sometimes viewed in a fatalistic way, but habits can be changed at any time! All it requires is the choice to do better and then about 21-40 days of willfully acting on that choice to make the wise decision automatic. It will be something you have for the rest of your life!

Sometimes focusing on doing something better can feel overwhelming, but when you weigh three to six weeks versus the rest of your life the investment is small considering all that can be gained. Even working at improving yourself can become a positive habit of its own.

It all begins with actively making the choice to do better.

85

This week I heard a few comments from children like "I wish I were like so-and-so." Wishing is fine if it is meaningless. However, I think one of the biggest ways we deceive ourselves is to compare ourselves to others, judge ourselves as deficient, and then try to be someone we weren't created to be. We will never be happy, nor can we achieve our full potential, by trying to be someone we're not.

Yes, looking at what makes others successful (or not) can be beneficial. I also believe it is good to have heroes and to emulate qualities that will help us bring out the best in ourselves. But it is destructive to actually want to *be* someone else, or to ignore what makes us wonderful.

Ultimately, nobody will ask me, "Why weren't you Michael Phelps?" But if I fail in being true to myself, they will certainly ask, "Why weren't you Matt Wunderlin?"

86

I want to wish your family a very Merry Christmas. Every year at this time it seems like there is an excitement, or an anticipation in the air. We hear people talk about the "magic of Christmas," or "the holiday spirit," or "the spirit of giving." And yet, often times, when the time is complete, there is a sense of disappointment and unfulfillment.

I have often heard of the sense of let-down once the season is over. Not that visiting the family was bad (or all bad anyway), not that people's generosity wasn't wonderful, and not that there wasn't something different in the air. Somehow our expectations of what this time of year is about is unmet, so then we either look forward to next year or develop a sense of bitterness or callousness about the holiday.

For most people, the reason is simple: What this time of year is really about *was* unmet. This season is not about giving or receiving gifts. It is not about getting the family together for a big meal. It is not about some sort of ethereal spirit. It is about a baby in a manger, Emmanuel, "God with us." This season exposes our innermost longing to be with our Creator, but when that is dismissed as fantasy, or replaced by consumerism or some other idol, our whole being protests.

When the greatest gift of all is forgotten, ignored, or put too low on our priority list, we remain unfulfilled. On the other hand, once the truth is discovered, the joy of Christmas never leaves us.

87

Thank you for another great week of swimming. The children are working hard (and hopefully having fun) as we enter the last month of the season.

It is a good time for your children to ask themselves, "Did I do what I wanted to do this season?" "Did I reach my goals?" "Why or why not?" "What could I do differently?" "What can I do for the rest of the season to get the most out of my time?"

Some may not have had a destination in mind when they began. If they did not, I would think it difficult to find a purpose in practice. Others may have had to change their goals along the way. Others may have had a season beyond their wildest imagination. Be sure to take the time to reflect upon what you've learned, while there still is a chance to do something about it.

More importantly, take the time now to reflect upon your life and make changes while there is still a chance to change something. All too often I have met people who feel they are stuck in their circumstance. That is usually not true. Usually they are enslaved to something else that makes them feel their circumstances are necessary, and, more often than not, that slavery has to do with money.

There is freedom in Jesus Christ, so that you don't have to accept what your sinful self created. When you give your life to Christ, you are free from the power and the penalty of sin! It may still be present, but now that the victory is won, you hold in your hands the key to freedom.

88

This week I want to set the foundation by explaining the difference between motivation and dreaming or desire. I also want to talk a bit about our role as parents.

We all want motivated children – they do better in everything – but motivation seems elusive. Sometimes we think our children are motivated, but then their actions don't reflect their wishes. I see motivation as a consistent internal drive that leads to action.

I was sure to put "that leads to action" because without this second half we do not have motivation; we have a desire. Let me explain what I mean by contrasting desire and motivation. A swimmer may have a desire to swim at the state meet. A motivated swimmer has that desire. They set their alarm clock and wake you up so that you can take them to morning practice. An athlete may dream of getting stronger. A motivated athlete rides his bike through the rain to lift weights. A student may want to go to a good college. A motivated student budgets her time so she can study, and she spends time researching universities in the library or online. I hope you see the difference.

I also want to be sure you see that motivation is consistent and internal. Ultimately, if the child doesn't want it, there is nothing we can do to motivate them to go after it. However, that does not free us as parents (or me as the coach) from helping them develop motivation. This is the difference: I want all of our swimmers to be consistently motivated to swim at their maximum potential.

But the athlete may not care about that; they just want to swim for fun while occasionally being motivated to improve. However, even though they aren't motivated consistently the way I want them to be, the lessons that I teach them in swimming should carry over and help them find motivation for something honorable. I have the responsibility to help produce drive, but they must choose where that motivation leads them. Your role as a parent is even more influential – in fact, nobody will influence them more.

Therefore, we want to be sure we are doing our job as parents. Remember, I have three children so I'm in this boat as well! And we must *be* their parents. Too often we stray to the extremes of either being overprotective or else absent. We should know where our children are at all times. We should have rules that they follow. We should know their friends. We should forbid drugs and alcohol. We should let them make mistakes and reap the consequences, but be able to step in when necessary, to keep them safe. We need to spend time with our children and listen to them, but also give them space to do things without us. We need to let them figure things out for themselves, but provide guidance. In short, we have a balancing act! But the bottom line is that we have to train them to grow into independent and respectable ladies and gentlemen.

89

I was thinking a little bit about excellence, in particular why excellence is often unreached. I came to the conclusion that, just how excellence isn't achieved in a day, it also doesn't disappear in a day. I think that the most common culprit is compromise on little things, or making things that are very black and white into shades of gray.

Let me give an example. There is a correct way to do a streamline. It is fairly black and white. A streamline is either done correctly or it is not. One of the ways that a streamline is done correctly is by intentionally squeezing the arms against the head. It may make you an eighth of an inch longer and a quarter of an inch narrower. But it takes effort to squeeze. The shades of gray start to come in when an athlete starts justifying reasons why they shouldn't do it correctly. "It makes me more tired" or "it doesn't make that much of a difference" or "nobody will notice" are three examples of false justifications. So, the athlete compromises.

Now, a coach can't see on the deck if an athlete got an eighth-inch shorter or a quarter-inch wider while they are underwater. Hence, the athlete gets away with it. They may even hear "good job," because it seems they are doing it correctly.

But they are not. They have compromised. After you compromise once, it is easier to compromise again. As long as an athlete is within a certain range and putting forth a certain level of effort, it is difficult for coaches to tell if they are truly giving 100%. They get away with being a second slower in a set and selling themselves short. Then they flip turn a little slower and get away with it, because we can't perceive a couple of tenths of a second.

Maybe they catch an extra breath when they shouldn't have or didn't push a stroke or kick as hard as they could have.

It all adds up. On the surface it appears that the athlete has done everything exactly the way the coach as told them. But they haven't. They have made black and white into a shade of gray.

It will catch up with the athlete in meets, of course, but it is even possible to continue to improve while compromising. However, that athlete will never reach his or her full potential and will always miss excellence.

Now think about how this applies to life, school, careers, and morality. Isn't this how we let sin take over?

To think, it all started with a compromise that seemed insignificant.

90

It surprises me that some people still believe that talent is an innate characteristic. Science has overwhelmingly shown that for 95% of the population, you have the potential to become a great success at your chosen endeavor – swimming, business, chess, music, art, etc.

Even when you take a look at the elite superstars you often find they weren't the most gifted, that is, others who had more genetic aptitude didn't go as far. Sociologists conclude then that you don't have to be the smartest; you only have to be smart enough. You don't have to be naturally good; you only have to be naturally good enough to even become world class. And most of us fall into that "good enough" category in one area or another.

So, we all have the potential to be world class in something. After that, it's just hard work, right?

Actually, that isn't quite right. After all, very few of us personally know someone who is truly world class at something. Yet we all know people who have, by all measures worked hard for 10, 20, 30, or even 40 years in a field. Some of those people who have spent decades in a career or hobby may even be below us in their aptitude.

The difference is "deliberate practice." The people who excel to the world class level don't just work hard – they work hard on purpose. Their purpose is to get better. They are constantly analyzing and trying to improve areas where they are lacking. They look for ways to get better. It is more of a cerebral function than a physical one – even in a sport like swimming!

And their efforts are exhausting. To be intently engaged is difficult when our minds would rather wander. What's more, it takes about 1200 hours of deliberate practice to be above average at something. It takes over 4000 hours before most would consider you an expert, and it takes 8000-10,000 hours of deliberate practice to be truly world class in any endeavor.

Is it worth it? I'll let you decide by considering another analogy.

A bar of iron is worth about $5. That same bar of iron deliberately worked into horse shoes is worth about $10. That same iron deliberately worked into sewing needles is worth about $3,600. When formed into springs for precision watches, the same piece of iron is worth over $250,000.

The iron didn't change. The iron's potential didn't change. But what was deliberately done to the iron made the difference 50,000 fold.

91

This season our theme is going to be "Every race. Every swimmer. Every time." A lot of people believe that our sport is about individuals, but really it is as much of a team effort as any other sport. I think it is important to remember that.

Why did Team USA do so well at the Olympics? Yes, Michael Phelps certainly helped, but he didn't win a medal in any breaststroke events, backstroke events, or long freestyle events. Also, an athlete can't get more than one medal in any event. We all have a place and no one person can be all things to all events.

Of the eight medals Phelps won, he probably wouldn't have gotten one without teammates pushing him in the pool every single day, and having guys like Ryan Lochte breathing down his neck. My high school coach used to say the most important person in the pool is the slowest swimmer, because IF that swimmer is chasing the next slowest he will work hard to not get caught. Thus that athlete will begin to catch up to the next person, who also doesn't want to get caught, so they swim harder.

Every child on our team makes a big difference. Every child plays a role in our successes. Though we have always done fine with supporting each other, we should build on that concept. It is important for the children to realize that nobody does anything great on their own. They need each other and they should support each other.

Often times only a few people, if any, get the glory, but even a ten-year-old kid swimming on a small United States Swimming team can honestly say, "I helped Michael Phelps win some gold medals."

Whatever successes Orcas have this season will be because of your child.

92

Blame it on what you will, last season we did not fill up our cookie water bottle. As you know, we have a large bottle that the children put water into whenever they have an exceptional practice. When it is filled up, coaches bring cookies to practice. For the first time since we instituted it, there was not going to be a cookie day.

I decided to have pity, and even though the children didn't earn cookies, I told them that we would have cookies anyway. I was also very clear that these were "grace cookies." I picked a day the last week of the season where I would bake an enormous number of cookies for the team. (By saying "I would bake" I mean "my wonderful wife would bake.")

I expected some children to come up to me and say, "Coach I can't be there that day can you save one for me?" or some discussions to that effect. After all, they are children and you can't blame them for trying to get a cookie. What shocked me was that I had parents contact me about their child getting a cookie on a different day because they were going to be absent on the designated cookie day.

This experience made me want to talk a bit about the importance of allowing life's natural consequences to occur. If you ask your child to do something and their first response is, "What do I get," then you should pay attention.

Life has a great rule in place; most of the time we get what we deserve. I'm not saying life is fair, but for the most part with all of the uncontrollables being equal, how you respond to something you CAN control will produce the results that you deserve. Motivated individuals know this is true. They focus on what they can control and use it to succeed.

What happens when we take this away? What happens when everyone gets a trophy regardless of effort? What happens when everyone gets an "A" just for showing up? Motivation decreases. Why bother putting in effort if I can be lazy and see the exact same result? There is no point in striving for more or trying to make things better. When we provide extrinsic rewards for everything, motivation cannot be internalized.

At the same time, we have to teach our children responsibility and help them to see what happens as a result of their actions. I personally believe that the loss of personal responsibility in our society is directly related to the false belief that people are "basically good" and that "everyone goes to heaven."

We need to expect our kids to do things and suffer the consequences when they don't. Children can set their own alarm clocks. Children can do their own laundry. More importantly, they can learn from the consequences of failing to do the above two examples without much harm being done. Better they learn this now than when they are in college or married!

If we constantly bail out our children or provide external rewards for responsibilities, they will have no need to become motivated. We must allow life's consequences to occur now while those consequences are small, so that later on when those consequences are large, our children will be responsible and motivated.

93

I t is evident that we have been working on our starts, turns, and streamlines the past several weeks. There were some amazing improvements and a lot of great efforts. It was exhilerating to watch your children move closer to their goals.

When we think about our goals, there is always action implied. There is always something that we need to do to make it happen. Good habits will not come by themselves. Good character doesn't just happen by chance. Hard work doesn't just appear out of nowhere.

While pursuing a dream, we have to be aware of the tendency to ask how to go about it, when we know it perfectly well. We must take the initiative; stop hesitating, and simply BEGIN. We must be resolute. We must say, "I will go to morning practices," "I am going to revise my resume," or "I am required to do that task today."

The actions that lead to our goals must become inevitable.

I think most of us know the above it true. It sounds nice and courageous written in this letter. In fact, it is courageous to do this and we admire those who do. Yet, we have one more excuse. It lurks in the shadows until the moment we choose resolve. Then it plunges forth to steal our ambition.

This excuse is the seemingly rational phrase, "I'll begin just as soon as…" "I'll start running just as soon as the weather warms up." "I'll look for a new job just as soon as the kids get older." "I'll tell my boss my great idea just as soon as this project is finished." "I'll quit this sin just as soon as…"

The problem is there is always another apparently rational "just as soon as." So it doesn't happen. Then, despair can set in. You can feel trapped or feel things will never change. You may even falsely feel like YOU are destined for failure or that you can't do anything right.

The trick to prevent our dreams from being swallowed by this excuse is to remember: We have to take the initiative where we are. We can never take it from where we are not.

We need to get rid of "just as soon as" so we are only left with the proper phrase, "I'll begin."

94

Employers have noticed over the past decade that employees believe they should be promoted and get pay raises simply because they show up to work. Regardless of what type of work they do, there is a sense of entitlement merely for doing the minimum. The same employees also tend to quit as soon as the going gets tough, instead of following through with responsibilities. Experts believe that adults who have no motivation, who have little or no connection between quality and rewards, are the result of a childhood of unearned rewards instead of working towards true achievement.

In the 1980s, there was a great deal of research on self-esteem. Subsequently, there was a great deal of hype in the media connecting self-esteem (defined as feeling good about yourself and seeing yourself as smart, funny, nice, etc.) and achievement. As a result, nearly all schools and affiliated extracurricular programs began programs to improve self-esteem. However, those folks, hyping and utilizing the research, committed the fallacy of confusing the cause with the effect.

In the 1990s, follow-up research clearly showed it was not self-esteem, but a realistic sense of self, that is most important. The mistake made in the 80s was that those interpreting the data looked at high achievers and found they had great self-esteem. They assumed the success was the result of high self-esteem. However, the follow-up in the 90s proved that the good self-esteem was because they achieved. It was not the cause of it! But this research did not get touted in the same way. After all, everyone loves the "feel-good moments," which explains why most people are still on the "improve self-esteem to produce high achievers" bandwagon.

This way of thinking is a motivation killer. Healthy competition and a desire to win or improve are critical to motivation. Why be motivated if you can get the same reward for being lazy? Part of the reason communism failed is because those who did a good job were rewarded exactly the same as those who did work of a poor quality. (My wife can attest this from her life experience having grown up in a communist country.) You can't win, if there is no opportunity to lose. Additionally, regardless of where you go in life, or what career you choose, there is going to be inequality. It is important to be able to deal with that, too.

There must be opportunities for accomplishments and for true excellence in order to produce the desire and motivation to achieve.

95

There are two major points that I think are important for developing motivation in our children. I am sure there are many others, and since you know your children better than anyone else, I'll leave it up to you to discover them.

The first point is that we must be careful about the friends our children make. We know that our children's friends greatly influence them. Unfortunately, we know that they tend to reduce themselves to the lowest common denominator. As such, it is important to know those friends and to set boundaries over who influences them and how much. As developing humans, they cannot do that on their own because they have no reference point.

Motivated people usually surround themselves with other motivated people. Your child's friends should be people who want things in life and who are positive influences.

The second point is that you need to help your children find meaning and purpose in their life. Doing things like studying the Bible and participating in volunteer work are important, but there are other critical aspects. Talking about family and personal values is very important. We cannot expect kids to figure it out for themselves when they turn 18. We need to raise our children up in the way they should go so that when they are older they will not depart from it. Listen to your children's ideas, but correct their reality if necessary. Let's face it; some things really are not as good as others. Talk to you children about their decisions and how it relates to their values. Does it reinforce them or conflict with them? Finding meaning has a lot to do with consistency between actions and words.

Purpose and meaning in life should be our greatest motivators. We do not want our children wandering aimlessly. They will make some mistakes, but they don't need to make all of them. As a parent, it is your biblical duty to help keep your children on the right track.

96

One of the marks of most people who live ordinary lives, that keeps them from being extraordinary, is what I call an "avoidance ethic."

The term, avoidance ethic means that an individual tends to set standards based on what they didn't do, as opposed to what they accomplished. Their behavior is often based on a list of don'ts, and they judge others and themselves by how well they avoid the things that they consider "bad." All too often, their favorite vice doesn't make the list, because we all have excuses for our own selfish behavior.

Part of the reason that avoiding trouble, forbidden behaviors, or uncomfortable situations impresses no one, is because it is expected of everyone. We don't admire Olympians because of what they didn't do; we look up to them because they went above and beyond. Your boss won't give you a raise because you did the minimum expected. Your teacher doesn't give out A's because you weren't tardy. Coaches don't praise you because you didn't goof around.

Not doing wrong isn't the same thing as doing right!

People who are motivated, who live out values, and who make a difference in the world, look at the positive side of things. Sure, they have things they avoid, but they raise the bar by also considering actions that must be done in order to succeed, like waking up at 5:00 in the morning for practice or bringing sack lunches to the homeless.

One of the easiest ways to see how you fare is to look at the things you say to yourself. Extraordinary people tend to ask questions like "What can I do to make this happen?" or "What sacrifice must take place?" Those content with getting by, who avoid things of lasting value, tend to ask "What can I do to avoid problems?" or "How can I be more comfortable?" or "What's that got to do with me?"

Are you avoidance-oriented? Do you compare yourself to others, or gossip? Putting others down to make yourself feel better is an indicator that you're not on the right track.

How do we defend ourselves to others at home, work, school, or the pool? Those with the ruinous avoidance ethic ask questions like: "What's wrong with what I did? I swam the whole way." "What's wrong with this project? I did what they asked." "What's wrong with only putting my dinner plate in the dishwasher?"

The better way to think about our behaviors, and the way that leads to lasting success, is to ask questions like "How can I do this the best I can?" "In what ways can I do this better next time?" or "What can I improve on right now?" "How can I help others while I take care of my business?"

Remember, there are two types of sin: There are the sins of commission – doing something wrong. And there are the sins of omission – not doing something you should have. It is the latter we all too often ignore.

One final way to think about why the avoidance ethic never leads to success, is by using the almost clichéd analogy of a bank account. When you do positive things, you add to your bank account. When you do negative things, you withdraw from the account. When you base your life around avoidance, you won't overdraw your account with negatives, but you also won't put in any positives. Your balance perpetually stays at zero.

97

Have you ever noticed that things always seem like they have a way of working out? We Christians refer to this as God's sovereignty. When I reflect upon my life, both in and out of the pool, it is interesting how things that seemed almost tragic at the time, often led to great triumphs, or how something that seemed insignificant, turned out to change my life.

I never would have met my wife if it weren't for a series of tough disappointments. I never would have become a part of the Orca family if it weren't for the minor decision to come in and swim laps one particular morning.

Though many people don't take time to look back as often as they should, it is easy to connect the dots in hindsight. However, it is next to impossible to connect the dots while looking forward.

Oh, we try, and we are occasionally successful. But more often than not, we just have to trust. Most of the time, we are given just enough information to get through our present circumstances. There is a lot we need to concern ourselves with in the present – to worry about the future is distracting and unhelpful. We can only control aspects of the current moment.

With swimming, the head coach (me) tries to orchestrate the big picture. Seldom do we do anything without some specific purpose or goal in mind. I am bringing this up because this week I got a lot of the "why" questions. I love answering the "why" questions, and it is normal human (especially child) behavior to want to know why.

But sometimes the many "whys" can interfere with practice, and so there must be trust. Often times, we can only provide the children with enough information to get them through the moment. We keep the big picture in mind and have many tools at our disposal to move your children towards that big picture. We love curiosity about our sport and this message isn't about squashing that, but sometimes too much of the "why" question is unhelpful (and sometime I believe it is a deliberate stalling technique).

By the same token, even the simple curiosity of "what are we doing next" or "what are we doing tomorrow" is a bad habit IF the athlete is supposed to be concentrating on improving in the current moment.

By being in the moment and trusting, we can make the best impact on the future. In that time we will be able to look back and connect the dots and see why everything happened the way it did.

Praise God that he is the "head coach" of our world and our life. I pray we learn to trust and avoid bad habits.

98

I want to talk very briefly about the difference between "being there" and "showing up." In swimming, "being there" means coming to practice – having a physical presence. But that doesn't mean the athlete has actually shown up. "Showing up" is when your *entire* being is there. It is when you engage a practice with your mind, as well as your body.

Often times, children who are physically located at practice for a majority of the time don't improve. They may wonder why. If I press them and ask if they actually "showed up" – left their troubles at the door, did the practice as they were supposed to, and deliberately worked on ways to improve – the answer is negative.

Sometimes, people still don't understand the distinction. Usually the following two examples make it clear. Husbands and wives can "be there" with each other but if neither "show up," their marriage is usually in jeopardy. Parents can "be there" by spending time with their children, but if they don't "show up," a bond doesn't form. We can all point to examples of times we didn't "show up" as a parent or a spouse. These are lost opportunities.

If someone or something is important to you, it is not enough to just "be there." You need to "show up" if you are to make a real difference.

99

This week I had the opportunity to visit my friends Adolph and Joyce Kiefer. Adolph won the 1936 gold medal in the Olympics and, of the few thousand races he did at the International level, he only lost twice in his career. Following that, he wrote a learn-to-swim program for the military that taught over two-million armed forces members how to swim. Since more troops died of drowning than bullets, this program saved countless lives. After that, he and Joyce founded numerous companies, including the Kiefer Corporation, which is one of the largest suppliers of aquatics materials in the world. At the time of this writing, Adolph (age 92) and Joyce (age 90) still go to work every day.

Besides being nice people, one of the reasons I love visiting the Kiefers is because of the perspective they bring to life, now that they are nearing the end of theirs. While they regale me with tales of their life (I don't talk much while visiting them for fear I'll miss some entertaining story or tidbit of wisdom), I can't help but see an underlying current that has motivated them throughout their lives. That current is the quest for significance.

When we think through our lives, I think most of us can also see how the desire to be significant is a common thread. As babies we were significant simply for being. However, it didn't take long before we lost a sense of importance about ourselves. So we began a lifelong struggle to find meaning.

As toddlers we were relieved that everything we did was special. "Look, I can crawl." "Now I can walk." "See how fast I can run!" But, soon we realized that those special things weren't so special after we did them on a regular basis. So we sought out other ways to stand out and win praise and feel accomplished.

We worked hard in school believing that our good grades were meaningful. At first they were – until they became expected. Then we endeavored to learn an instrument or play a sport. At first the challenge of becoming an average player was enough to demonstrate importance, but it didn't take long before that wasn't impressive.

Next we began to look outside of ourselves for that feeling of distinction. "How do I compare to you when I do X?" And we felt good while winning or gaining applause or getting our name in the newspaper, because for a while we felt significant again. It seemed like being the best at something was the route to go. Our goal is to reach the top of the hierarchy of whatever we find important (and often we selfishly define what is important based on what we are good at).

Unfortunately, many people stop maturing at this point. Once they can't win medals and ribbons, they try to have the biggest house or the fastest car or the earliest retirement. They gossip in an attempt to feel better about themselves by putting others down. They judge others by pointless things like how nice their lawn is or the type of clothes they wear. Whenever they feel a lack of meaning, they seek escape in alcohol, drugs, or lust. In short, those stuck in comparisonitis waste their lives.

The next stage seems to be finding significance in helping others. We move beyond trying to one up others, and instead attempt to build up others. We focus on our children and our friends. We devote time to charities and churches. We find significance in the betterment of humanity. We also realize that Zig Ziglar's proposition rings true, "You will get what you want if you help enough other people get what they want." In general, we respect people in this stage as being wise and mature. They are "good people" in our minds. Some may even mature to the level where 99% of their motivation is truly altruistic - save for the tiny desire to feel significant.

But what happens when you've gotten everything you've ever wished for? What happens when everything you thought would make you happy doesn't? What do you do when you realize the world is going to move on without you? What is the value of significance when your significance is forgotten?

The Kiefers have done it all. They have a large and loving family. They made millions. Adolph was the best on the planet at what he did. He literally changed the world and made it a better place. He worked hard and reaped the rewards of a charmed life – and graciously shared those rewards with others. Where is he now that he is 92?

He realizes that significance doesn't lie in what you did. It doesn't even lie entirely in who you are, as most people in the world will never know you. In the beginning, we had it right all along. Our significance lies in simply being. What matters is that we matter. We were created out of wisdom and love – a wisdom and love so great that we cannot impress it, nor can we do anything significant compared to it.

An atheist can find no meaning in life despite the many things they do, because they reject this Creator.

Nominal believers who think God belongs to one hour on Sunday, and who think salvation comes from baptism or a church membership, don't understand what God is. Those who simply believe that "God is love and tolerates everything and everybody goes to heaven" reduce WHO God really is. Both groups think their meaning lies in what they do (hence STILL trying to make themselves the significant ones).

Every other faith outside of Christianity taps into human pride and tries to get us to earn our significance.

But Adolph is a Christian and finds true meaning in spite of everything he did, and finds everlasting peace in grace that originated in the most insignificant of times and places.

100

This week, I reflected on what it means to do well, and that led me to another of our Orca values – Sportsmanship. As I was processing my thoughts, a very simple explanation of what "sportsmanship" is about dawned on me: Sportsmanship is all about the adverbs. That is, the spirit BEHIND all of the things we do matters more than the concrete results. Example #1 – She arrogantly walked toward the swimming blocks. Example #2 - She humbly walked toward the swimming blocks. The verb in these two examples is the same; it is the adverb that separates being a lady from being a punk.

Living well and being a good sport is about living the ordinary life and doing the ordinary things extraordinarily well. Too often we believe that cleaning the kitchen, commuting to work, feeding the kids, shuffling papers, etc. leaves us with no energy or time for "real living" – and yet these mundane acts are a majority of everyone's existence, and how we approach these acts determines whether or not we are truly enjoying life!

If you can't live well with the way things currently are, then you can't live well at all – no matter how much success or failure falls your way. Example #1 – He grudgingly accepted the pay raise. Example #2 – He graciously accepted the handout.

I don't need to mention again how fortunate we are here in the United State. We all have blessings and curses in our life. But ultimately, the *one* thing you always have responsibility for, and control over, is your attitude. If you want to be extraordinary in your ordinary life, then you must begin by seeing that which is extraordinary hidden behind the mundane (and sometimes the pain). Then, you must make a habit of seeing it.

The Orca team sincerely hopes that we are helping your child realize this so they can *live* like a good sport. Example #1 – He regretfully looked back at his life. Example #2 – She fondly looked back at her life.

101

This week as I was talking to one of your children they said something that struck me, "I'll try harder." We always refer to practice as "training" and not "trying harder." We define training as "practicing what you are going to do in a meet." Training is necessary because it prepares people to do the right thing at the right time for the right reason. But this is not the same thing as trying harder.

In swimming we see people try harder all of the time, but they never get any better. If you have an inefficient stroke and just try to swim faster, you may actually go slower. Instead, you need to train to do the right thing, which, in this case is having correct technique. If you try harder on flip turns and do them too far away from the wall, you fail because it wasn't done at the right time. If you try harder, so your start is perfect and at the right time, but isn't aggressive, you fail because it wasn't the right reason.

Much of our frustration in life is from trying to manage things that are beyond our direct control. We try harder, but we do not train. When we flip on our car blinker to change lanes and the person behind us speeds up to cut us off, we get angry. We say that we need to try harder so that next time anger doesn't consume us. But the next time the same thing happens.

Instead, we need to train ourselves in patience and grace, so that when such an incident occurs we are ready to do the right thing at the right time for the right reason. If we are proud and boastful, we need to train in service instead of trying harder to be humble. If we are greedy and worried about money, we need to train ourselves in generosity and simplicity. If we are depressed, we need to train ourselves in celebration.

The best way to attack vices is to train in the opposite virtues. It is true in swimming and it is true in life.

Tidbits That Didn't Make My Top 101 Letters

-Just as the water provides us with a reflection of our physical self, so the sport of swimming can provide is with a reflection of our character: discipline, responsibility to others and self, dealing with winning and losing, handling fear, confidence, trying new things, challenging self beyond what is comfortable, perspective, goal setting, positive self-talk, honoring a higher power, how to relate to others, integrity, and many others.

- I truly believe that a hero is not someone who just does great things – but someone who sacrifices and does great things despite not necessarily wanting to. And being a hero doesn't mean that you're not afraid; more often than not it is doing the right thing especially when you are afraid.

- If you believe the naysayers, it makes the naysayers right 100% of the time. But the funny thing is that when you don't believe them, you are right more often than not. The greatest achievements of humankind were done against someone else's "better judgment". But even if you fail, you are still more successful than you otherwise would have been.

- Albert Einstein once said, "Try not to become a man of success, but a man of value." A person of success may still have a life that lacks meaning, but a person of value is always successful. Our team's primary goal is to help you instill these values in your children. Champions and world records come and go, but character lasts a lifetime. Swimming and other sports do not have much value if they do not strive to create young ladies and gentlemen of character. I look at swimming as a tool, not an end. It is a tool to help mature your children into respectable adults.

- An interesting study was once done on horses. They took two separate horses and measured how much weight they were able to pull individually. Then they put the horses together as a team and measured how much weight they could pull. One would think it was the total of the individual pulls, but it wasn't. It was almost four times that total. Teams can accomplish far more together than what individual efforts would indicate.

- I want to encourage you to get your child to practice as often as you can, and if they simply "don't feel like it," please give them the extra nudge so they learn about the responsibility of being on a team. Dedication is not based on how we feel.

- Often times we artificially limit ourselves, and that is our only barrier to doing something extraordinary.

- I believe that happiness is partially the result of being a part of something bigger than oneself, and that doing charitable activities fosters that happiness.

- Training the mental side is just as important as training the physical side. There was a great study done which proves this point. People were told to shoot free throws with a basketball a certain number of times. The results were recorded. Then the group was divided in half. The first group actually practiced shooting free throws. The second group visualized shooting free throws. Then they repeated the free throw shooting trial. Both groups improved equally well. As the mind believes, so the body achieves.

- Though there is often trepidation in doing something different from everyone else, I believe there is a lot of truth in the following saying: "If you do things just like everyone else, you end up being just like everyone else." We should strive to do them better.

- It is often been said that "success is a habit" and that the key to success is "getting comfortable being uncomfortable." This weekend we saw the result of practicing well (being successful in practice), and of courageous children (doing things that were uncomfortable). These types of actions do carry over into other areas of life, which is one reason why our sport is so great.

- When everyone matters you can be a contender.

- My thought has always been that I want a team I am glad my own children are on.

- At the end of the day, service matters infinitely more than trophies and ribbons. Being on a team allows us to be a part of something greater than ourselves, and it allows us to do things greater than we ever could have done on our own.

- There is an old proverb that says, "There are two mistakes one can make on the road to success, not going all the way and not starting."

- Vince Lombardi once said, "Individual commitment to group effort, that's what makes a team work." We appreciate everyone's commitment to attending practice.

- Some food for thought as we go forward, knowing that the children have rededicated themselves to doing well for the remainder of the season: "The miracle is not that I finished. The miracle is that I had the courage to start." Too many people fear failure (or success), so they pad themselves with the (supposed) comfort of "if I never had the opportunity to give my best, I never really failed." This excuse is a lie, and usually everyone sees it, including the person telling the lie. We all have the opportunity to succeed, and failure by definition is not trying. How can anyone fail if they have given their all and grown in the process?

- This past week marked the half-way point of the year. Are you where you want to be? This is a good time to reflect on resolutions and goals, and to rededicate yourself to excellence.

- In sport, as in life, we are on a journey. During any trip there are going to be smooth roads and pot holes. If we always focus on the potholes, the trip isn't very much fun.

- God gave us flowers to enjoy, but without the mud around them they wouldn't grow.

- In the end, nobody's obituary contains information on how well they did in age-group sports. It talks about character and the people they love. Age-group sports can help you develop honorable character if it is done intentionally. It won't happen on accident.

- Sometimes minor setbacks occur. It is important, however, to not turn one bad thing into two bad things. Don't make two bad things into three because of a bad attitude. Use what you have been given, and what you gave yourself, to move forward as best as you can. Don't ruin a season of training because one thing didn't go perfectly.

SPEECHES

THE ORCA WAY

While the Orca Way is something that is hard to define (most parents describe it as a feeling of acceptance or love or community or that every swimmer, regardless of talent, matters), I hope that this description of our five values will begin to impart a sense of what it is about.

Spirit: I think this one is the key. All things start from within—thoughts become words; words become actions; actions become habits; habits become character. Our thoughts must be rooted in love for one another, our opponents, and our community—regardless of how we are treated in turn. If we get this right, the rest of the Orca way is easy.

Sportsmanship: Nothing leads to our internal decay faster than things like envy, boasting, arrogance, and rudeness. If we are selfish and insist only on doing things our own way, we become intolerable (if we always get what we want) or irritable (if we don't). While these things are easy to recognize in others, they are difficult to see in ourselves. We all have an excuse for every selfish thing we do. These must be rooted out. Then, we can be gracious in winning and honorable in losing.

Dedication: We must be patient and kind. By patient, I don't just mean put up with practice times and be devoted to the team during the honeymoon-like portion that comes with all new things. I mean that we must be patient in the hardest way, with who others are. After all, a team is made up of individuals with many quirks and flaws. True success in this area comes when you can be kind to everyone, not out of some sort of obligation, but because you want to accept everyone on the team.

Motivation: We must be motivated to do things correctly. We don't want to be motivated by resentment, or happy that we have done something well, when others do wrong. We should do our best and not squander our gifts because that results in honor to our creator and a true sense of personal satisfaction.

Excellence: We have seen that when the above values are aspired to, excellence is reached. Perfection can never be obtained, but excellence can, even if you can barely swim across the pool. Personal bests are more important than medals. Virtue and character are more important than personal bests. When excellence is attained, it carries over into all aspects of our life. But it starts and ends with agape love.

FLOSS

(This talk was my version of the popular "Sunscreen")

As a swim coach we get many opportunities to talk to the children about lots of things outside of swimming. The only thing is that most of the time, your children's brains are so oxygen-starved that they don't hear or they deliberately ignore us. Therefore, I've attempted to put the collective wisdom of our coaching staff into one quick speech in a situation where they have to listen.

My first, and probably best, piece of advice is this: be sure to floss. Pretty much everything else I'm going to say is not based on anything but my opinion. But the benefits of flossing have been proven time and time again. You'll live longer and spend much less time under a dentist's drill.

Enjoy the power and beauty of your youth. Oh, wait you probably have no idea what I'm talking about. But trust me, in 20 years, you'll look back at yourself and recall, in a way you can't grasp now, how much possibility lay before you and how wonderful you really are.

You are stronger than you think. You are smarter than you think. But you are less wise than you think.

You have more potential than you could ever believe. If someone were to tell you all that you are capable of, you would not waste your time on anything that didn't prove beneficial. And you certainly wouldn't waste your time on waiting for life to just happen to you.

Don't worry about the future. Don't dwell on the past. You can't change the past and the future is all made up. The real troubles in your life are going to be things that never even crossed your mind, the kind that surprise you - like when coach's realize that you're the only one in the relay who can swim fly. So, focus on the moment. Live in the present. And always do your best.

Do one thing every day that scares you. Or else coach will put you in an event you've never swam before.

You didn't chose to be born in this country, to your parents, with the gifts you have and the struggles you have, in this period of history, with your skin or eye or hair color, and with your intellect or lack thereof. More importantly, realize that nobody else chose those things either. Give of yourself when you can, and let others help you. A gift can't be given if you won't accept it.

Sing. Nothing will make you happier than singing. Unless coach is talking.

Knowing what is right is fine, but learning to do what is right is what matters most. So stay in the pool until everyone else is done racing. Then shake their hand.

Sometimes in swimming, as in life, there is going to be pain. Sometimes all we can do when you hurt is to tell you to keep going. But if it gets worse, make sure you tell someone.

Challenge yourself to be better. Every day just improve 1/10 of a second. It adds up quickly.

Learn to forgive others and have mercy on them. Ultimately, that will help you more than them.

There are two kinds of people in the world: Those who do the work and those who try to take the credit. There is less competition in trying to be a doer, and doers sleep better at night.

Don't waste your time on jealousy. Sometimes you're ahead, sometimes you're behind. The race is long and, in the end, it's only with yourself. Coaches care more about personal bests and you having a good race than they do about what place you took.

There is no faster way to depression than only seeking your own happiness. Your worst enemy is not pain and suffering, rather it is boredom and selfishness. These lead to self destruction.

Remember compliments you receive. Forget the insults. If you succeed in doing this, tell me how.

It is nice to be gifted, but it is more important to be a gift.

Leave everything better than you found it. You are a guest here.

Have respect for others. Everyone can't be the same if we're to be successful. There is always going to be someone better than you at something. There is always going to be someone worse than you at something. And you never know when they'll be on your relay.

Get plenty of calcium. Be kind to your knees and shoulders. You'll miss them when they're gone.

Beware. BEWARE. Someday when you are in college or somewhere else, someone is going to make you feel like you've been brainwashed your whole life, and that you need to learn to think for yourself. Then, they are instead going to teach you to think like they do, not for yourself. Don't confuse that.

Five words will separate you from everybody else, and help make you successful: "I'm sorry. I was wrong."

Remember that your parents changed your diapers. They got up with you in the middle of the night and comforted you while you were crying. They drive you to activities and to be with your friends. They've spent hundreds of thousands of dollars raising you, and even more minutes than that worrying about you. So, on your college essay when they ask you "Who was the most influential person in your life," don't say "My best friend Tiffany who I met 3 weeks ago." Get to know your parents before they are gone. Parents do the same. Don't mistake driving them to activities and buying them frivolous stuff with being a part of their life.

Turn off the TV, video games, and the Internet. There is a real world out there waiting for you to be a real hero.

There are a lot of people who feel like they live their life in chains, and they wait for others to try to free them. What most people don't realize is that they are the ones holding the key. Give yourself the freedom to do something great.

Don't sweat the small stuff. A messy room, getting a "B," losing a race, or having a bad hair day are not disasters. Just ask the people suffering in the Sudan.

Believe in something bigger than yourself. Be a part of something bigger than yourself. Do things that you won't get credit for. Sacrifice for the team; others are counting on you.

Success does not come from what you do, rather from who you are. Someday you will not have races, tests, or even a job. Nobody will care if you went to state or not. Nobody will care what car you drove or what size your house was. The only thing that will matter is who you were and how much you loved and gave of yourself.

Be nice to your siblings. They're your best link to your past and the people most likely to stick with you in the future.

The most important decision you will ever make in your life is who you are going to marry. Don't settle. Once you choose, make the same choice again every day so you don't wake up one day with a stranger. Life is better enjoyed with two.

Friends will come and go, but you need to work hard to keep friends – and it is work - because the older you get, the more you need the people who knew you when you were young.

Respect your elders. Speak only the truth.

Honor those who made the sacrifice to make our country one of the only places where you can freely complain about our country. The best way is by respecting our pledge, our flag, and our anthem.

About truth, realize that a lot of what it called "science" right now will prove to be untrue before you die.

Hands on the wall, feet on the bottom, mouth closed, ears open. You have two ears and one mouth. Life will treat you better if you listen twice as much as you speak.

Don't mess too much with your hair or by the time you're 40 it will look 85. In other words, you've got to shower after practice.

People have a right to complain, but you have a right not to listen. Don't listen to anyone who tells you that you are not capable of something. If you believe them, they're always right – but if you don't you'll always be better off.

Don't read beauty magazines. They will only make you feel ugly.

Dance, even if you have nowhere to do it but your living room.

Read the directions, even if you don't follow them. But always follow coach's direction.

Don't buy things you don't want in order to impress people you don't like.

Don't be so busy taking care of your children and providing for them that you forget to spend time with them. The saddest thing I hear as a coach is, "I wish you were my dad."

Take personal responsibility for everything that happens to you. There is no greater failure than the person who is never at fault.

There is such thing as truth. One belief or opinion is NOT just as good as another. Some things, like the Bible, are true whether you or anyone you know believes it or not. So don't flutter kick while doing butterfly or you'll get disqualified.

Don't believe the garbage that "Once upon a time nothing exploded and became everything. Then against the laws of physics assembled into the most amazing things you've ever seen. Next dirt became alive by accidently forming self-replicating machines so complicated that we can't even begin to understand it. Those cells then became apes which then became your grandpa." You are not an accident or an animal. You were created by God for a purpose.

Work with disabled people whenever you get a chance. They will show you how handicapped you are.

You can get everything you want out of life if you will just help enough other people get what they want.

Freedom is found in two places only: Simplicity and the ability to make a wise decision.

Have fun and enjoy life. If you wouldn't do something for free, it MAY not be worth doing. BUT remember that there is joy and pride to be found in working hard. It is the process NOT the result that truly defines you. And character gets built by doing things that you need to do but don't necessarily want to do. So please, please, please make it a point to floss.

CLOUDY

NOTE: This was written after my wife and I suffered a miscarriage during a championship swim meet.

It should have been cloudy yesterday. I mean, that's how it is supposed to be when your child dies, cloudy. But it was sunny. In fact, it was beautiful outside. At first it makes you wonder if God cares at all. I know what the Bible says, that God loved us so much that his son Jesus died on our behalf. I know that if we ever seriously examine our self we know that we don't deserve salvation—even if most of the time I don't feel like I'm all that bad. But Jesus still died and rose again so that whoever believes in him may have eternal life. But this was God dying for the ultimate purpose, whether you believe it or not, or whether you feel it or not, it is simply the truth. And, even then, it was cloudy.

However, ours was not even 17 weeks old. What could possibly be the purpose? I would have thought that God, if he exists, could spare a drop of rain. But there was nothing but blue sky.

I mean, we already started making plans for this baby. And we imagined how he or she (we don't even know) would interact with Sierra, Bryce, and Titus. We were picking out names. We were picking apart our lives to know how the baby would fit in. We even planned for the weather around his birth. It was supposed to be sunny then, not now.

17 weeks is just too short. About all he had time to do was get my wife, Reka, sick and moody and make her back ache. I had to take care of her. This was our first pregnancy with any major symptoms, so I really had to learn patience…and how to be generous with my time…and how to be kind…and how to be more understanding…and how to be a lot less

selfish. I guess I also learned to feel some sympathy for all those other women out there for whom pregnancy is more of a trial. Not to mention their husbands.

But, one thing I didn't worry about, the one thing I didn't do very much of, was prayer for this child. I just assumed it would be fine. When a miracle happens to you three times in a row, it is easy to forget that it is a miracle. I guess I learned I need to rely on God more. After all, he can take that miracle away. I suppose I also learned to be more empathetic for others who have felt this loss. It is no longer intellectual understanding, it is real to me.

And what about everyone else? It isn't fair to lose a brother or sister. Though, the kids are dealing with it really well and their sadness instantly left them when they realized the baby was in heaven. Sierra even said that we now have someone to look forward to meeting when we go there. Bryce just wanted to know why God didn't bring the baby back alive. "He could," I said, "but he won't." Maybe my faith isn't as strong as theirs.

This one's passing sure made me realize how much I love them. I should never take them for granted.

Reka's family was devastated, probably even more than we were. Their world view can't explain this type of tragedy. We found ourselves comforting them. Maybe this baby will ultimately bring more people to Christ than I did—intellectual arguments and a good testament only go so far. It truly takes a movement of the Spirit...and sometimes the boldness that only comes with tragedy.

It is comforting because my family and friends have been praying for us. Though, I sometimes wonder when people say that if a prayer ever gets uttered. This time I am less dubious. I don't often cry in front of others.

You really realize how much you are loved when others come to you in a time like this.

When Reka first started bleeding, we prayed together. I was glad that before we even knew what was going on she prayed for God's will to be done. If she hadn't said it, I probably would have. But it wouldn't have been sincere. I wanted my will to be done. And now, I want rain and clouds.

We prayed a lot. Sometimes we feel awkward praying together. Not this time. Maybe awkwardness comes from my wanting to always take care of things and handle them. This time I couldn't. I was so lost I didn't even know where to begin. I have never felt so helpless. I never before realized the depth of my sin and how little I can offer God as a bargaining chip. In fact, most of the time I couldn't even speak a prayer. But it was sincere and honest silence…then prayer flowed as things got worse.

Prayers were answered last night. As Reka and I sat together on the couch we both realized a certain closeness. It wasn't two days earlier we were talking about why God often seems so hidden and why he never seems to feel present. And suddenly, there He was. We felt a supernatural peace and love, joy in the midst of suffering. It wasn't denial, the pain was still there. It wasn't making ourselves feel something to help us cope. It was real. God was not hidden. I don't know how to put it to words; it has never happened to me before and it may never happen again.

If you'd have asked me before which miracle I prefer, I would have chosen Bryce's without hesitation. Now I realize that in 17 weeks this baby has served God's purpose in many ways, and will continue to do so. It may have done more in its death than I ever did in my prideful life. I think now the miracle of God showing up is greater than the miracle of bringing the baby back to life. You can't imagine how great God's love is until he shows up like He did while Reka and I mourned on the couch.

Maybe that is what God was trying to show me with the sunshine all along.

COACHING PHILOSOPHY

Some thoughts on my coaching philosophy:

1) I must be myself because I can't be anyone else. I am outgoing but not emotional. I am agreeable, but passionate about the truth. I am educated and intelligent, but will never know it all so I devote at least 30 minutes per day to education. I will not compromise my principles, but I will always listen to what people have to say. I am not a good salesman. I am not good in the bad cop role. I value swimming only in how it develops children, by itself (besides safety) it is pretty frivolous. Winning means very little to me; doing one's best is the most important. I believe in taking responsibility for everything bad that happens on the team if I have authority to control the situation, but I need to make sure everyone else gets credit for the good. I need to not believe the hype about me, but rather the reality about me.

2) An athlete is not me. An athlete is not their parent. An athlete is not there to feed my ego.

3) Strokes must be taught as how they are most biomechanically efficient, and often this is different for different people, but almost always have common themes. Some people look at Michael Phelps and say, "Wow, he swam that 400 IM in 4:03.84! We should try to be like him." Because of my background, I tend to look at athletes and say, "Why didn't he swim four minutes flat?"

4) To best teach children, there needs to be a common coaching language, but things should be taught so that all learning styles can understand it.

5) To best teach children, there needs to be lots of repetition and revisiting of skills. As children's bodies grow, they need to often relearn things.

6) To best learn, children have to want to learn, and what they learn must be developmentally appropriate (children are not mini adults). Fear of reprisal changes behavior, and is useful for that, but it does not change motivation which must to taught to come from within (For example, police officers can get us to slow down, but not change our motivation about speeding). It will not come from within if the child is not having fun. Yet, at the same time, if they were only interested in having fun they wouldn't have joined a team; they would just go to open swim. It is no fun to be injured and a youth team shouldn't have very many injuries.

7) All coaches stand on the shoulders of giants. There are a lot of people who have done a lot of thinking that shouldn't be quickly dismissed. Much of what is popular today was the technique taught in the early 1900s. Additionally, if USA swimming recommends a technique, there should be a good reason before it ever gets dismissed.

8) My job is to try to help the assistant coaches become better coaches than me and to make sure they never become scapegoats. "Why" and "how" are my favorite questions (from both coaches and athletes).

9) One of my main roles is a communicator - with parents, children, other coaches, and the board. I can't communicate if I don't know what is going on.

10) My role is that of a Christian servant leader to help children develop values and life skills through the sport of swimming. No job is too menial. No child is unimportant.

Some thoughts on my training philosophies:

1) Orcas is a new and growing team, so we are following a three year plan to develop the team enough so that, by the end of summer 2009, we can have a solid team base in different areas of the sport. Overall, we have stuck to the plan, even if it has meant that other team areas suffer in pursuit of the big picture.

2) A successful team/season must have a centralized training plan, so that macro cycle goals can be filled in meso and micro cycles.

3) USA Swimming's seven energy categories, when used appropriately, provide a beneficial framework for designing sets. These categories can be subdivided and one set may hit more than one area.

4) Swimmer improvement is most rapid when training is parametric. Parametric training is often too psychologically difficult for young athletes, so it needs to be broken up. Max Interval training will also produce results quickly, but must be used with caution to prevent injury.

5) Most parents and coaches want too much too soon, and thus, they limit their athlete's potential. Patience is a virtue, and our experience has been that, when we are patient, the children increase their potential and improve their times in the short term as well.

6) Most children today are catered to by their families and schools. This has resulted in less athleticism and a weaker mindset. This must be overcome, if we want to maximize an athlete's potential.

7) Children need to be with their peers. Children need to work with disabled children, so that they will learn how handicapped they really are, and how capable the disabled really are.

LEADERSHIP 101

Leadership is an elusive quality that many people believe is innate. They may believe it can be developed, but, for the most part, you've either got it or you don't. This is not true.

Leaders are made, not born. It only seems that some are born leaders because of certain characteristics they've developed throughout their lives. However, there are very specific stages in becoming a leader in any group. Once you are aware of these stages, you realize that God has given everyone the potential to lead.

I am going to refer to these stages using the names that I heard in my military training.

The first stage is called "operation." Operation is when you begin to learn the specifics of how an organization or group operates. On our team, it is knowing things like the practice times, our traditions and values, how to use certain equipment, and the rules. By rules, I mean both the spoken and unspoken guidelines for behavior. You cannot lead if you do not understand the basic principles which govern a group. To walk in and try to lead, without knowing anything about the sport of swimming or our team dynamics, is to create a barrier between yourself and the club. Once you understand the operation, you can move to stage two.

The second stage is called "cooperation." Cooperation is when you begin to support others on the team. You encourage your teammates and you challenge your peers to get better. You also work with the coaches to become better personally and to help the coaches improve the club. Additionally, you make sure everyone is included, as you try to prevent cliques from forming. This is also sometimes called the servant stage –

everything you do is about others and about the well-being of the group. If your motivation is self-serving, you will never be able to truly advance to the next stage.

Stage three is called "leading by example." This is self-explanatory; you must be a good follower before you can be a good leader. Here is where you truly attain the trust and respect of your peers. It is not enough to encourage them to get to practice on time if you are always late. To lead by example is to do the workout to the best of your ability, to take initiative in all aspects of the club, and to demonstrate integrity (do the right thing when nobody else is looking). Often times, this stage overlaps with stage two. However, stage two must come first, because an athlete may not be capable of stage three unless they've spent some time in stage two. Swimmers will definitely not be able to move to stage four unless they've spent significant time leading by example.

The final stage of leadership is to "lead by voice." The athlete is now a leader. They will declare things, and their peers will listen to them and do what they ask. These are the team captains, whether they are officially in that position or not. There is great responsibility in this stage, because if you fail at this level you will go all of the way back to stage one. Since people will do what you say, choose your words wisely. Since people will copy you, be worthy of emulation. Since people will look up to you, you must develop the next generation of leaders.

In the final stage of leadership, there are certain other things expected of you which you may not have anticipated. The first is to delegate responsibility to others. You can't raise up other leaders if they never have the chance to prove themselves. The second is to define problems clearly. You can't just say "this stinks" and gripe about it. Once you've specifically defined the problem, you should immediately help with the solution. Everybody has criticisms; leaders have ideas. The third thing you need to do is act positively even if things don't work out. Nobody will follow a negative person for long. You must be purged of the victim mentality if you want to be a leader. The fourth thing is to turn "why" into "how" and turn "they" into "we." Instead of bemoaning why you have to deal with something, look at how you can change it or use it to your advantage. Instead of looking at why others may have an advantage, or why "they are so lucky," look at how we can do it better or overcome. You can only shoot the bullets you have.

The process of becoming a leader is not as ethereal as one might first believe. In order for a team to be effective, it must develop leaders so that 20% of the group is leading in some capacity. Once you know the progression you can tap into your God-given potential and make a difference on the team.

PYRAMID OF SUCCESS

Welcome to the Orca season! We are very glad to have you with us. This season our motto is "Orca helping Orcas." We want to be a team where we build each other up in all areas of life. No matter who we are, we all have something to give, and we all have areas where we can greatly improve. By working together as a team, we can all grow together and at a faster rate than we ever could on our own.

I thought I would begin this season by presenting you a brief overview of what I call the "Orca Pyramid of Success." I will say that the Orca Way (Spirit, Sportsmanship, Dedication, Motivation, Excellence) are sort of like the air all around the pyramid. Like air, it is often in the background and not necessarily noticed unless reflected upon, but it is vital for there to even be a pyramid.

At the base of the pyramid is you, the parents! Regardless of endeavor, you have more influence on your child's success than anyone else (you've already given them genetics and taught them 90% of everything they'll ever learn in their life). When they get older they may not want to admit that, but it is still true. You might think that what coaches do is the most important thing for your child's swimming success. That is simply wrong. It is what you as a parent does.

Some examples: On Orcas we do not make practices mandatory, however, the more practices a child comes to the more successful they will be. For most children, they simply can't physically come to practice without you. Their success in the sport is largely due to your commitment to getting them to practice – even if they don't feel like it. Giving in to "I don't feel like it" would excuse them from embracing challenges and enduring hardship, and teach them that commitments are only valid so long as they feel nice. Plus it undermines the development of common goals and collective rigor which underlies all successful teams.

Children also will copy your attitude. If you are frustrated with their swimming, they will become frustrated. If you focus on effort (which Orcas recommends!) instead of position relative to others, they will focus on that. I could go on and on, but I hope you get the idea.

The next level of the pyramid is general health. This includes eating well, getting enough sleep, staying hydrated, having time to relax, and other day-to-day things that are essential to a balanced life. Again, much of this is dependent upon you and your attitudes and actions, but a lot of it is also about teaching your children to make good lifestyle choices. For example, if a child eats poorly, their "engine" can only run so efficiently and thus performance is limited – in all areas of life!

Ok, now at the third level of the pyramid, we coaches begin to have some real influence (we can talk about general health, but are not in a position to implement it). I would call the next level "metabolic conditioning." It is the balance of training between aerobic and anaerobic workouts. Put more simply, it is how the different workouts go together at the cellular level to make your child fit. Coaches spend a lot of time coming up with a detailed plan to help benefit your children. I don't believe in doing any type of workout without a specific purpose behind it. However, lack of practice attendance and the like can disrupt this plan. A child's lack of effort can disrupt this plan. Lack of general health can disrupt this plan. There is some advantage to showing up no matter how infrequently or what the effort is, but you need to ensure that expectations and hopes match the realities of how your children fit into the plan for metabolic conditioning.

The fourth level of this pyramid is strength. We are going to spend more time here than we have in the past, as this is where our team seems to be the most deficient. Our sport is all about being able to apply force on water, walls, and starting blocks. And nearly all swimming races are all out sprints, so the more force that can be applied, the better the athlete will perform. One thing that I want to encourage all our middle and high school athletes to do, for instance, is to sign up for the summer weight lifting program that the school district offers. I have spoken at length with the people that run the program and I can't think of an athlete on our team who wouldn't benefit greatly from more strength.

The fifth and final level I will simply call "sport." This includes things like learning proper technique and repeating many repetitions of correct movements. Sport is an application of fitness (levels 3 and 4) which is an application of base levels 1 and 2. When good athletes train, they train with a purpose to better some aspect of their performance. After doing this thousands of times (sorry, there is no quick road to success that bypasses the seemingly mundane aspect known as "correct repetition") they become great athletes. Probably more so than any other sport, the quality of each repetition is vitally important in swimming because even Olympic caliber athletes are at most 10% efficient in battling the resistance of water. Added to that, our sport only has a small variety of repetitions that are performed. There must be mental tenacity to be a good swimmer. It takes a lot of brain power to concentrate on the same motions over and over again, constantly fine tuning and making correction. So first the athlete must learn what must be done, then they must do it, then they must make sure they are doing it their very best each time, and finally, they have to do it repeatedly. That is sport.

These five elements working together will determine how far your child can go, and hence, we call it "the Orca pyramid of success." The Orca Way determines what they as a person will look like once they get there.

SWIMMING FOR LIFE

Somehow we never expected that things would turn out this way. All too often we dream, or even anticipate a happiness that we may never feel. But we also find joy and peace in that which we never imagined...or sorrow when it was least expected. One thing is certain – we are no longer what we once were. That is part of the journey.

I want to use the next few moments to take you on a journey by drawing a parallel between coaching and parenting, and swimming and life. This certainly isn't a historical account, nor is it making a prediction. However, I hope you will find that it is true.

A coach begins planning long before the swimmers arrive. Before the season is birthed, we create hopes and plans and dreams for the athletes, and for the team. We see potential. We see obstacles to overcome. And like preparing for a new child to enter into the family, we think we know a lot more than we do and everything looks great on paper. Somehow, we know the road will be long, but at that moment the fatigue isn't real and the giants are easier to slay.

Then comes the first day of practice. It's nice in swimming that we can call it "practice." There's a little more pressure that first day a child is born. The reality of the early days is that we didn't expect there to be so many diapers. Regardless, practice is about training and learning new skills and preparing for big days or races. We put so much energy into our plan, hoping things will come out the way we dreamed.

And it doesn't take long before we realize our detailed plan may be closer to an outline than we first anticipated. And there is a sense of frustration, and dare I say stupidity, in trying to push forward on a road that sometimes feels like it may lead to nowhere. But in spite of all our deficiencies, confidences, wishes, hope, and progress occurs. We may have a state champion yet.

But the season goes by way too fast. The children grow. Soon they will be racing. Soon we won't be able to do things for them. Soon they'll have to do the best they can with what they have and with what we gave them. For better or for worse, some of the things we couldn't or wouldn't fix along the way, we learned to tolerate.

Then, usually later, though with sporadic instances in the present, we regret our tiredness, the time away, the time we could have invested more, or the time we made mistakes. But we are still too much in the thick of it to act effectively on it. Surely we will not even notice most of what was lacking until hindsight takes our opportunity away.

And so the season of testing begins. We try to give our swimmers advice before they step up onto the blocks. We coaches are also nervous, and hope unsolicited advice will compensate for missed instruction. Though, deep down we know that only habit will prevail once the pressure is on.

We give the advice anyway hoping something, anything will stick.

Then the race starts. We can't go back and change the past. We hope the athletes will remember what we've taught them. We hope our swimmers will look to us for advice and act on it. We see mistakes. We are surprised by triumphs. But if we were involved, and if we truly got to know the child, they perform, for the most part, exactly as we expect – when we are being realists.

Almost as soon as it begins, the race ends. How we react to the athlete tells us a lot about who we really are. How a parent responds to the success or failures of their responsibility speaks volumes about him and his relationship with his child. Some coaches see their athletes merely as a way to elevate their ego – they are often passionate and angry. Some see their swimmers merely as a duty to be taken care of – they are often indifferent. Some cannot separate themselves from their athletes – their athletes are smothered and often can't reach their potential because they haven't been given the necessary freedom. There is often an identity crisis. Some coaches simply love their swimmers, take them where they are at, place responsibility where it belongs, and strive to do better together next time, while celebrating the moment.

At last, the season ends. We all know it wasn't supposed to be forever. Then an athlete becomes a coach. The child has children of her own. But we still see the little girl, though she is a grown woman. While we want to see the simple loving heart she had as a child, she will have moved on. Yet, she will have learned from us. She will pass along many of our failings. She will also give the next generation our successes. It will begin again.

By that time, our fatigue and our stress will be a distant memory. We will realize that if we would have slowed down and spent more time with our children, the giants really were easy to slay. But we can't return and replace the time we had. Instead, we will try to help our child avoid the mistakes we made. We will try to compensate for our lack of investment – this is why grandparents are accused of spoiling their grandchildren.

We hope our children will listen to us now that they are adults.

We also fully realize why people don't visit their parents, and hope we weren't guilty of the greatest parenting crime, found in this axiom, "If you want your child to spend time with you when you are old, you must spend time with them when they are young." They won't remember that we worked overtime for their new game or a bigger house. Nor will they care.

Just like athletes don't remember coaches for the hours they spent writing workouts and reserving pool space behind the scenes.

Before long, Time will unleash its awesome responsibility, and we will be removed from history as we enter history. There will be no more dreams of happiness left unattained. It will all be long ago in a swimming pool that is no more.

But the ripples in the water will go on, if we were dedicated to our swimmers. In the end, there will be no end, if we give of ourselves to a child.

Orcas, never forget, we love you and your moms and dads love you.

LONG AGO

Wow, it is hard to believe that the season is already over. There were times this year when it seemed like we would never get to right now – when we were right in the middle of things, trying to balance our time, trying to get through one more practice, looking forward to the moment when a dream would be realized, not knowing if we would succeed or fail.

In those moments we look to the future for strength. We look at the present as the only reality. But we seldom think about how now, right now, will all too soon be a long time ago.

Parents, you know exactly what I mean. Look at your children. There is no way they should be as big as they are right now. It was yesterday, maybe a few days more, that we were changing their diapers, and now they come downstairs and argue with us about "what is that you're wearing."

I mean, wasn't it just a week or two ago…maybe a little longer…that we had to push them on the swing, and when they got tired of walking, we picked them up and held them in our arms – kind of annoyed. And yet, is there anyone here who wouldn't give just about anything for one of those unashamed hugs, or those moments when *we* were all that they needed.

I guess it was only about a month ago, or maybe it was slightly longer, you were keeping your child away from the swimming pool because it was dangerous - they couldn't swim. How is it now that they are better in the water than we are? Remember how proud you were the first time they jumped to you off the side of the pool all by themselves? It's already a long time ago. Those moments shouldn't go away so quickly.

But they do. So don't let another slip away because you're "too busy," or working so that you can have more stuff or a house that's too big anyway. Soon *now* will be long ago, and you will want this time back . . . Well, most of it anyway.

Swimmers, my little Orcas . . . and some of my big Orcas who were little when we first met, you need to realize that you do not have all of the time in the world. It seems like this will go on forever. But it won't. It seems like there is always a next time or another season or another practice to reach your goals. But there isn't. Each day that passes, each moment that passes, either brings you a little closer, or a little farther away from your dreams.

And guess what? Someday, very soon, you will be just like us. And 33, or 40, or 50 won't seem old to you the way it does now. Because it will be *your* birthday. And it won't seem like it was that long ago that you were in the pool, trying to move water, trying to go faster, trying to get better...or not. Because maybe you weren't in the pool for that reason. But when you are 33 or 40 or 50, you'll wish that getting better was your reason.

Because you will look back on yourself, as you are right now, and you'll see how much potential you have. You will see exactly how great you are and how much opportunity you have at this moment. And you will say of yourself, "As long as I had a lane, I had a chance." But then, it will be no more. And 33 or 40 or 50 is not that far away, and right now will be a long time ago.

But even if you never are an Olympian or never even make it to a state meet, you will have benefited. You may not know why you seem to be more dedicated than most to family or your studies or your career. And you will be proud of the fact that you stick with things when others would quit. You may not know why you find motivation to do difficult things or to resist temptation when others fold. You may not know exactly why you treat failure and success different from most. You may not understand why you can't settle for doing things "good enough." You will not quite understand what makes you a success where others fail, even if life doesn't treat you fairly – because it won't.

The reason you succeeded, even if success just means persevere, will partially lie in what you did a long time ago, in a crowded pool, with a group of people whose names you may not remember, but whose faces you will never forget.

People have said to me, "As a coach you get to be a hero to a lot of kids." But that isn't true. I get to work with a lot of heroes. Some of them are heroes today, and some will be heroes tomorrow. All I did was help them move water.

All too soon these days of moving water will be a memory. But what you learned along the way will not. You probably will not even remember what you learned and when you learned it, but it will always be a part of who you are.

And so you will wake up one day at 33 or 40 or 50 and realize that it was not you who moved the water, but all along it was the water that moved you.

Final Words from Coach Matt

What would you do if you knew you only had an hour to live? We've all heard those silly questions about what would you do if you had a year to live, or a month to live, or even a week to live.

But what if you knew you only had an hour. I thought about this, and I realized that I would probably spend my first 45 minutes calling people and telling then that I love them and saying goodbye. I also wouldn't hesitate to tell them the truth about the gospel and about Jesus. I wouldn't apologize for doing this either.

What would I do with those last 15 minutes? I actually spent a lot of time thinking about this recently. Probably more than what is practical, because, really, I'm not going to know when I have 15 minutes of life left.

Anyway, I thought about it, and I know what I would do. I would do the dishes. No, really, I would do the dishes. I'm not talking about loading the dishwasher and pressing the button. That would be a waste of the last fifteen minutes of a life. There comes a time when technology takes away from existence.

I would fill up two sinks – one with soapy water, and one with rinsing water. Then I would put out the dish rack and have a couple of drying towels nearby. I would gather my family and we'd do dishes.

Some might think I'm crazy, but if you have 15 minutes left to live you want to do something meaningful and valuable with it, not fritter it away. So, I'd do dishes with my family.

Why, you ask. I think that in those 15 minutes, I'd be able to tell my children and my wife everything that I'd want them to know, everything I'd want to teach them in 10 years.

The first thing they'd learn is that it is okay to be silly and goofy. "What, you're dying? And you're going to do the dishes?" They'd think I was nuts. But then, they'd realize it is okay to be a bit off your rocker, and not take things too seriously.

The second thing they'd learn is that it is important to do things together as a family. It really doesn't matter what it is as long as you are together.

Third, my wife, my standard of beauty, would know how much I love her. She hates doing the dishes. I don't mind. I would do it for her so that she knows how much I love and appreciate everything she does for our family.

Fourth, this would teach my children not to leave a mess. Leave everything better than you found it. Nothing is so unimportant that this rule shouldn't be followed. Even if you're gone, someone has to deal with any garbage you leave behind.

Next, it would teach my boys that real men work and don't mind working and helping others. Too often they see on TV and in movies that the highest men can hope to achieve is to act like little boys. Real men sacrifice for their families. Real men worry about others more than themselves. And yes, real men do the dishes.

Sixth, it would teach my daughter that she should marry a real man; not someone who is perpetually a little boy. Anyone who'd get drunk or go skydiving or fix up their lawn to impress the neighbors isn't worth her time.

Then, I would make sure that I splash the kids. They need to remember to have fun. If you're not having fun, it might not be worth it.

This would also teach my wife that it is okay if everything isn't in order. It is okay not to be perfect, and to waste time. Even if you've only got 15 minutes left, we need to have fun. But then we'd clean it up.

Ninth, as I wipe off the old food, I would remind my children that these dishes are just going to get dirty again. Life is always getting rid of the old and replacing it with the new. Right now our children are the new, but one day they will be the old. Don't forget that you will die. Death is our greatest gift, because it reminds us to take advantage of life. Enjoy your meals before they become the old food that is wiped away.

Finally, as my last few minutes ticked away, doing the dishes would remind everyone that it isn't too late to make a difference. You're not done until you're finished. You're not finished until you are dead.

And even if I didn't do the best job up until that point, those dishes would be the cleanest ever.

EPILOGUE

Dear Reader,

Shortly after assembling this book, my family and I moved away from our beloved Waunakee. We left many friends from our church and my swim team. This caused me to realize two notable notions.

The first is that we often don't celebrate and show appreciation for the people we care about until they leave. We have parties and encomiums for friends when they retire, move away, or die, but seldom do we show them our gratitude while in the thick of things, while there is still time to bond and enjoy one another. For some reason, it is difficult to express admiration for a person when we see them often. But, if we truly want to connect with people, isn't the most obvious time to venerate them while we are together? Now, I am not saying that people should have celebrated and appreciated me more; rather, I regret that I did not demonstrate this enough to the people around me.

The second realization I had upon moving is that many of my stresses were petty, and they generally came in three forms. All three varieties could have quickly been solved if I would have acted on them in a timely manner, leaving behind only those stresses which truly needed my concentration.

The first form was those tensions where I let something eat away at me, instead of simply confronting a person about how I felt. Most of the time, even if that person is somehow your competition, that individual would not want to harm you as an individual. By burying my pain, I planted negativity and allowed it to grow far greater than the original offense. I should have communicated how I felt and forgiven from my perspective, offering it up in prayer. And even if the offending individual was lacking morals to the point where they didn't care what their actions or words did to me, talking to the offender in a non-threatening manner would have improved the situation. It would not have resolved all differences, but it would have made things more cordial.

The second form of stress was those areas where I should have compromised more. These pressures were items that didn't really matter, but I chose to dig my heels in despite how it made others feel. These are difficult to see when you are involved, so the counsel of a mentor would have been invaluable (I personally believe it is imperative that *everyone* be discipling somebody while being discipled by somebody). When I felt anxiety about an issue, especially when someone else approached me about changing, I should have brought that before an individual or group of individuals more mature in the Christian faith than I am. It was only pride that led me to believe I could handle the decision myself, or to believe that I was always right.

The third and final stress was those things that simply were not real. Whether I made up something, or listened to too much hearsay and gossip, I spent excessive energy being concerned about the make-believe, or those things possibly based on reality that never came to pass. Oddly enough, I have counseled people, many times, to focus their energy only on those things they can control, and then to trust in our sovereign God. Yet, only in hindsight do I realize how often I did not trust God with those things. Quite simply, this reflects a lack of faith and a lack of prayer on my part.

So, to summarize my insights, we need to love and appreciate people more while we are with them. We also need to let go of our pride and approach others when they hurt us, be more forgiving and compromising when we are approached, seek advice from others, and pray that we can trust God more when we are anxious.

Simple, right? As with everything written in this book, on paper it seems easy. Because the truth is that the concepts are easy! Putting it into practice is far more difficult, which is why we need to find true biblical fellowship, so that we can stay on the narrow path. We all need constant reminders, people who can hold us accountable, and people with whom we can share our trials and tribulations. Life in isolation is shallow, and to believe you can be independent of others *and* successful is foolishness.

Please pray that I will take my own advice.

Humbly,

Coach Matt

CPSIA information can be obtained
at www.ICGtesting.com
Printed in the USA
LVOW11s0224230318
570931LV00001B/32/P